The Book of Forms

LEWIS TURCO, born in Buffalo, New York, in 1934, is Associate Professor of English at the State University College, Oswego, New York. He received his B.A. at the University of Connecticut in 1959 and his M.A. from the University of Iowa in 1962. He has held poetry fellowships at Yaddo, Bread Loaf, and at the Writers' Workshop of the University of Iowa. Mr Turco is the author of three books of poetry: *First Poems* (1960), *The Sketches* (1962), and *Awaken, Bells Falling* (1968). He was the founder, and for three years director, of the Cleveland State University Poetry Center. In addition, Mr. Turco has contributed prose and poetry to many journals, including *The Atlantic Monthly*, *The New Yorker*, *Poetry* (Chicago), *Saturday Review*, *American Scholar*, *Kenyon Review*, *Paris Review*, and *Sewanee Review*. His poem "November 22, 1963" has been widely reprinted in this country and translated abroad, and it serves as the basis for a ballet "While the Spider Slept," performed by the Royal Swedish Ballet.

The Book of Forms

A Handbook of Poetics

LEWIS TURCO

New York   E. P. Dutton & Co., Inc.   1968

SBN 0-525-47209-6

For Vern and Mort and,
in some ways, better days.

Contents

Introduction

The Book of Forms: A Handbook of Poetics is intended as a text and reference work for students of poetry in general, and of verse composition in particular. Although the accent is on the forms of poetry, this volume contains all the information essential to the student of contemporary poetics.

In addition, *The Book of Forms* has a number of unique and unusual features:

I. "Some Notes on Metrics" is a chapter that surveys the various prosodic and metrical systems, clarifies such terms as *rhythm*, *cadence*, and *meter*, and provides clear explanations of the processes and methods of versification. At the end of the chapter there is a table that lists the symbols used in the schematic diagrams of the various verse forms set forth in Chapter Four.

II. The chapter entitled "Some Notes on Sonics" begins with a concise definition of the poem as a series of levels—"visible," "sonic," "sensory," and "ideational"—that, taken together, form a "fusional level" of interrelationships. From this point, the chapter proceeds to a discussion of the techniques of the sonic devices of poetry—such as rhyme, elision, alliteration, etc.—that were not covered in the first chapter.

III. The concern of Chapter Three, "Some Notes on Tropes," is with figurative language and the various aspects of what was once called "wit" and, more recently, the faculty of "fancy"—allusions, symbolism, metaphor, irony, and so forth. The chapter concludes with a discussion of the various kinds of "ambiguity" in poetry.

IV. Chapter Four is the heart of the volume. It is really a book-within a-book; therefore, it is titled, "The Book of Forms." It is divided into three parts:

1) The first part of this chapter is a "Form–Finder," in which all the forms contained in the volume are listed and divided, first into *regular* poem and stanza forms, and then into *irregular* forms. Under *regular forms* there are further subdivisions, beginning with *one-line forms* and working through *two-hundred-ten-line forms*.

Should a student wish to know the form of a poem he has been studying, rather than leaf through all the forms in the book, he may first determine a) the *rhyme scheme* of the poem or stanza in question and b) its *meter*. Then he may c) *count the lines of his form* and turn to the Form-Finder. There, under the appropriate heading, he will find a short list of stanza and poem patterns, which he may investigate in order to determine the exact name of the form he wishes to identify.

Similarly, should a student of verse composition wish to attempt a form of a specific length, he may use the Form-Finder to discover an interesting structure. Many students find that there is no quicker way to improve as writers than through formal experimentation and attempts to solve specific technical problems.

2) The second section of Chapter Four is intended to be the most comprehensive rehearsal of the verse forms that are *traditional in Anglo-American prosody:* over 175 specific forms are listed alphabetically.

Our heritage of forms is very rich. We are heirs not only of British metric systems, but also of systems derived from Europe, the Middle East, and Asia. Our history of verse forms goes back through the Normans, the Anglo-Saxons, and the Celts, and we have derived much from the systems of the Hebrews, the Greeks, the Italians, and the French.

The verse forms here set forth have all been utilized at one time or another by poets of the British Isles and North America. During four periods of the history of English letters, particularly, poets have used and extended the forms here described. During the Middle Ages, the Renaissance, the Romantic, and the Victorian periods, and throughout the twentieth century—but particularly the contemporary era—there have been craftsmen who have explored the possibilities of the formal structure of verse.

True as this is, to this point no attempt has been made at a systematic survey of our traditional forms *in toto*, and to make them all available, in as clear a manner as possible, to students, student-poets, and the poets themselves.

Chapter Four is just such an attempt, and it contains a number of features that no other volume at present offers:

A) A *unique* schematic diagramming system for all forms. By studying the diagrams one can see readily the structures of the various forms.

B) *Concise* prose descriptions of the forms.

C) *Complete* cross-references, so that students can discover relationships and similarities among many of the forms.

An additional word ought to be said on this last subject: while researching these forms, the author has discovered ambiguities in many of the descriptions set forth by his sources. He has also found that in several cases distinctly different forms have been lumped under one terminology or another. In order to clarify the study of verse forms, in some cases the author has invented the names of forms, but in every case these inventions are *derived from the original ambiguous terminology*. In no instance has a form itself been invented. On the other hand, a number of the classical forms have not been used in English poetry, and these have been excluded from consideration, as have some invented forms— such as the Clerihew or the many varieties of sonnets other than the major forms. However, invented forms, like the Keatsian ode, that have passed into the body of our tradition are fully covered. Some forms, such as the line invented by Ogden Nash or the contemporary eighteen-line accentual poem—pioneered by William Carlos Williams and adopted by the younger poets—set forth on page 130, have not formerly had names at all, and nomenclature has been supplied as logic might dictate.

3) The third and last section of Chapter Four is a bibliog-

raphy of *contemporary* poems written in traditional forms. This bibliography has been included so that students may see, if they wish, how poets of today have adapted forms to our modern idiom and needs.

V. *The Book of Forms: A Handbook of Poetics* concludes with a "Glossarial Index" containing over 650 entries, of which there are three kinds:

1) Entries of technical terms, with page numbers, that appear in the various chapters and in the Introduction, with cross-references.

2) Entries for synonyms of terms found in *1)* above, with cross-references.

3) Definitions of various terms not covered elsewhere in the volume, with cross-references.

It will be seen, then, that the Glossarial Index is in itself a fifth chapter—a handbook in small—and it should be utilized as such.

LEWIS TURCO

Oswego, New York

Acknowledgments and Bibliography of Sources

The author wishes to express his thanks to Dr. Donald Justice, formerly Assistant Director of the Writers' Workshop of the State University of Iowa and now Professor of English at Syracuse University, for his early encouragement and advice; to Dr. Donald R. Tuttle of the Office of Education, U.S. Department of Health, Education, and Welfare for his critical suggestions and revisions; to Professor John Montague of the University of California, Berkeley, for remarks concerning the Irish forms; to Professor Philip Legler of Sweet Briar College for his encouragement in print; to Messrs. Fred Cogswell of the University of New Brunswick, Canada, and Alexander Craig of Victoria, Australia, for their early cooperation; to Professor William Keen of State University College, Oswego, New York, for suggesting the form-finder; to Professor Arnold G. Tew of Cleveland State University, whose help with the irregular forms was invaluable; to Mr. Dudley Fitts of Phillips Andover, Paul Engle of Iowa, Richard Eberhart of Dartmouth, John Ciardi of Bread loaf, and the many other poets and friends who have, at one stage or another, provided encouragement during the seven-year odyssey of this manuscript.

The author is particularly indebted to the various librarians associated with the White Collection of Medieval Literature of the Cleveland Public Library. They were of incalculable aid, as were these books:

Bridges, Robert, *Milton's Prosody*, Oxford: Oxford University Press, 1893.

Cohen, Helen Louise, *Lyric Forms from France*, New York: Harcourt, Brace and Co., 1922.

Davison, Edward Lewis, *Some Modern Poets, and Other Essays*, New York: Harper and Brothers, 1928.

Humpries, Rolfe, *Green Armor on Green Ground*, New York: Charles Scribner's Sons, 1956.

Justice, Donald, *Of Prosody: Notes for a Course in Contemporary Poetry*, Iowa City: privately circulated, 1959.

Knott, Eleanor, *Irish Classical Poetry*, Dublin: Colm O Lochlainn at the Sign of the Three Candles, 1960.

————*Irish Syllabic Poetry* 1200–1600, Dublin and Cork: Cork University Press, 1935.

Preminger, Alex, *Encyclopedia of Poetry and Poetics*, Princeton: Princeton University Press, 1965.

Untermeyer, Louis, *The Forms of Poetry*, New York: Harcourt, Brace and Co., 1926.

Williams, Gwyn, *An Introduction to Welsh Poetry*, London: Faber and Faber, 1953.

Wood, Clement, *Poets' Handbook*, New York: Greenberg, 1940.

Wrinn, Mary J.J., *The Hollow Reed*, New York: Harper and Brothers, 1935.

Chapter One
Some Notes on Metrics

Before one can begin to study the craft of verse construction systematically, one must understand something about rhythm, for rhythm is at the root of traditional English poetry. One of the basic functions of the poet is the *ordering of the rhythms of language*.

Three words must be defined before we can proceed further. The first is the word *rhythm* itself, and it may be defined as "The flow of cadences in written or spoken language."*

In order to go on to the job of ordering the rhythms of language, the poet must know the definitions of two other words: *prosody* and *meter*. *Prosody* may be defined as "The science or art of versification; specifically (a) The systematic study of metrical structure, including varieties of poetic feet and meters, rhymes and rhyming patterns, types of stanzas and strophes, and fixed forms. (b) A particular system or theory of versification or of metrical compositions; as Horace's *prosody*.

"The principal symbols for representing features of prosody are: ´ ictus or accent; · secondary accent; | a division between feet. Thus, My lóve | is líke | a réd, | red róse. In quantitative verse: ʋ– is for an iamb; –ʋ a trochee; –ʋʋ a dactyl; ʋʋ– an anapest; ––a spondee." Three other metrical units which sometimes occur are ʋʋ the pyrrhic; ʋ–ʋ the amphibrach, and ʋʋʋ the tribrach, and –ʋ– the amphimacer. The symbols used in scansion are ʋ the *breve* and – the macron. The virgule / is a stroke that is used to indicate a division between *verses*, not verse feet.

*Since one of the dictionaries most commonly used by students is the *Webster's New Collegiate Dictionary*, all the quoted definitions of words used in this section are taken from the 2nd edition (1951) of the *New Collegiate* published by the G. & C. Merriam Co., Publishers, Springfield, Massachusetts.

For the purposes of this book, the differences between the *primary accent* (ictus) and the secondary accent will be ignored. Instead, reliance will be placed upon a system that distinguishes only between the accented (–) syllable and the unaccented (ᴜ) syllable. Thus, an iamb (ᴜ–) consists of one *verse foot* containing two syllables: the first syllable is unaccented; the second syllable is accented. A dactyl (–ᴜᴜ) consists of a verse foot having three syllables, the first syllable being accented, the second and third syllables unaccented. We shall have more to say on this subject later.

To return to our definitions, *meter* may be thus defined: "Systematically arranged and measured rhythm in verse; specifically (a) The property of a verse that is divided into feet or syllabic groups. (b) The pattern of a verse marked by the prevailing foot and the number of feet."

To recapitulate main points, then:

1. *Rhythm* is *the flow of cadences in written or spoken languages.*
2. *Prosody* is *the science or art of versification.*
3. *Meter* is *the pattern of a verse.*

There are traditionally in English prosody four kinds of meters. Each kind has been called by other names, but for clarity we shall refer to them as *accentual, syllabic, accentual-syllabic*, and *free verse*. Strictly speaking, the last "meter," free verse, is not *metrical* (measured), for its nature is denoted by its name: the rhythms are *free* or *unpatterned*. For this reason it has been said that free verse is the most difficult of the prosodic bases, for the free-verse poet must have developed an ear for rhythms in order to keep from slipping from verse into prose. For further discussion of free verse and prose rhythms, see the section on FREE VERSE in Chapter Four.

Before discussing the other three meters, we must overcome one other word: *scansion*, and again we resort to the dictionary. To *scan* means "To go through (verse) foot by foot distinguishing the metrical structure."

Any kind of language, even prose, may be scanned. Thus, if you will note the marks above this phrase, you will see that it has been scanned into a series of five iambs, or iambic feet. Each syllable is either accented or unaccented in *normal* speech. Five iambic feet is a measure frequently found in English verse. It is called *iambic pentameter*, which brings up another semantic problem. Simply, *penta-* (from the Greek *pente*) means *five*. Thus, *iambic pentameter* means *a measure of five iambic feet*. Similarly, *mono-* means *one*; *di-* means *two*; *tri-* means *three*; *tetra-* means four; *hexa-* means *six*, and so forth.

Any of these prefixes linked to the word *meter* will denote a certain number of verse feet in a line of verse. By scanning the line it is usually possible to distinguish the *predominating* kind of verse foot in the line. Thus, *anapestic trimeter* means a line of verse in which there are three anapests, *or* in which there are *at least two* anapests, plus one other kind of verse foot.

It is important to note the last point: that scansion attempts only to establish the *normative meter*, for no true poet writes always in regular measures. When a person scans a poem and decides that the poem is written in iambic tetrameter, he is only describing a norm. Some lines may not contain even one iamb, but most lines will; moreover, in most lines iambs will *predominate*.

May we return for a moment to our definition of meter? Meter is "the pattern of a verse." It is only that—a pattern. One feature which distinguishes a poet from a versifier is that a poet *understands a pattern and works against it*, while a versifier *memorizes a pattern and works with it*.

There is nothing more monotonous than a regular beat carried over an extended period of time. Think of the metronome. But *counterpoint* (or syncopation)—rhythmical variation against a regular beat—contains the element of surprise, and handled skilfully, it can be most pleasing. When a poet establishes a metrical norm in his verses he sets into motion in the mind of the reader a regular cadence against which the poet will impose a series of rhythmical variations. If handled well, these variations will not seem dissonant (except for deliberately designed effects), but musically pleasing.

Such skill, however, is usually acquired only after much practice, study, and work: there is as much craft and understanding of technique required in the art of poetry as in any of the other arts. It takes patience as well as inspiration to be a bard, or *maker*, as the poet was originally called.

But we were discussing meters. The first of the three prosodic systems with which we have to deal is *accentual verse*. In accentual verse the only important metrical consideration is the number of *accented syllables* to the line. There may be any number of unaccented syllables in any given line of verse. For examples of accentual verse, see the sections on ANGLO-SAXON PROSODY, the PEARLINE STANZA, and the TRIVERSEN.

The second of the prosodic systems is *syllabic verse*. Here, the only important metrical consideration is the number of *syllables* to the line. There may be any number of stresses or accents in any given line. For examples of syllabic verse see the Welsh and Irish forms, the French forms, and the HAIKU, TANKA, and CINQUAIN.

The third system, *accentual-syllabic verse*, is the usual prosodic standard of English poetry. It depends for its basic pattern upon the more-or-less *regular alternation* of *stressed* and *unstressed* syllables.

Once again, it should be noted that these descriptions are descriptions of norms only, of patterns. For instance, in accentual-syllabic verse a perfect line of iambic pentameter will consist of ten syllables: five unaccented and five accented syllables alternated regularly beginning with an unaccented syllable. But the poet may vary this basic pattern in a number of ways: by substituting one kind of verse foot for another; by means of enjambment, caesura, and elision; by varying the quality and quantity of syllables. But these points will be taken up in the next chapter.

Some explanation must be given of the system of metrical notation which has been developed for *The Book of Forms*. The schematic diagrams that appear beneath most of the prose explications of these various forms, lines, and stanza patterns are designed to present visually 1) the number of syllables to the line of verse; 2) the number of accents to the line; 3) the rhyme schemes, and 4) the positions of rhymed and unrhymed refrains and repetitions. For these reasons, the traditional method of scansion is not used. Hence, the following symbols should be noted:

(x)	—Small *x* stands for an unrhymed syllable that is either unaccented or whose accent is unimportant;
(′)	—A slant stands for an accent (stress);
(x́)	—Stands for an unrhymed, *accented* syllable.
(a, b, c . . .)	—Small letters *other than x* stand for rhymes.
(á, b́, ć . . .)	—Small accented letters *other than x* stand for stressed rhymed syllables.
(A, B, C . . .)	—1. In the Welsh and Irish forms, capital letters stand for *main* rhymes.
	—2. In the French forms, capital letters (except *R*) indicate *rhymed refrains that are whole lines* or *repetons: whole lines that are repeated, but that are not refrains.*
(R)	—In some French forms, *R* indicates a *refrain that consists of only a part of a line.*
(A¹, B¹, A², B²)	—Numbered capital letters indicate *sequence of refrains.*
(or)	—In certain Welsh forms *or* indicates a syllable or word that *off-rhymes.*
(oe, ay, ei . . .)	—1. In certain Welsh forms, grouped letters (other than *x*'s and *or*) indicate *diphthong rhymes.*
(c, xc, bc)	—2. In certain Irish forms, a small *c* used alone or grouped with other letters, indicates *consonance*, not rhyme.
(xxx, xax, xxb)	—3. Otherwise, grouped letters indicate a *word* consisting of so many syllables.
(*x x a* x x)	—In the Welsh and Irish forms, *italicized* syllables indicate *possible positions* for

	rhymes, cross-rhymes, assonances, or alliterations.
(·)	—A dot stands for a *caesura* (or pause) in the center of a line.

If these symbols seem confusing out of context, they will become immediately clear once you turn to the schematic diagrams themselves.

There will be certain exceptions to these rules, but in each case the exceptions will be apparent and will be stated in the heading for each diagram.

Chapter Two
Some Notes on Sonics

A poem is a series of language patterns. The first and least important pattern is on the *visible level:* how does the poem look on paper? This is not irrelevant, for if one will compare how a poem by Walt Whitman looks in print, with the aspect of a poem by, perhaps, William Carlos Williams, one can tell the difference at a glance, perhaps even catch some impression of the unlike psychological effects these poems will produce on close reading. There is even one form, SPATIALS or *hieroglyphic verse*, that depends for its rationale on how the poem is set up in type.

Second, there is the *sonic level*, a much more important consideration: what musical or sonoral sequence does the poet weave?

Third, there is the *sensory level:* what mood does the poet evoke? What emotions, scenes, desires, and so forth.

Fourth, there is the *ideational level:* meaning, theme, philosophy, observation, moral.

Fifth, there is the *fusional level:* what does the combination of ingredients equal?

In this chapter we will deal with aspects of the sonic level that were not covered in the preceding chapter on metrics.

It has been pointed out that a regular rhythm repeated endlessly is monotonous. Since rhythm is a basic sonic effect, the poet must know something about how to vary his meters.

The primary analyzable methods of metrical variation lie in *quality, quantity, caesura, enjambment,* and *elision.*

QUALITY has to do with the substitution of one kind of verse foot for another, specifically of a verse foot different from the measure of the norm that has been established in the poem.

QUANTITY has to do with variation in the "length" of a syllable. The norm of a line of verse frequently establishes that the *long syllable sound* coincides with the *accented syllable.*

The substitution of a *short* or normally unaccented syllable for a long, normally accented syllable, and vice versa, constitutes a subtle method of rhythmic variation.

CAESURA is a rhythmic pause in the center of a line. The pause may be created by the manipulation of measures, by phrasing, or by punctuation.

ENJAMBMENT has to do with run-on lines. The normal expectation is that phrasing will be completed at the end of a line of verse or other metrical unit, such as a couplet or stanza, and that a pause or *end-stop* will ensue. Enjambment occurs when there is no pause at the end of the line and the phrase carries over into the next line.

ELISION has to do with the melding of two or more sounds into a single syllable or syllable sound. Bridges* has codified some of the analyzable methods of eliding:

1. *Vowels:* "When two vowel sounds come together, then if the first of the two has a tail-glide (a y-glide or a w-glide), there may be elision."

   a. Examples of y-glide:* come *fly*ing; *be it* so; *the oth*er men; *thee and* she; glor*y a*bove; *riot.*

   b. Examples of *w*-glide: *ruin*ous; *so oft*en; al*so in*; Maro*cco,* or Trebisond; fol*lowers;* sha*dowy;* gra*dual;* in*fl*uence.

2. "*H* is often considered as no letter." Examples: ought *to have; to her*self; on*ly who.*

3. *Semi-vowels:* "If two unstressed vowels be separated by *r* there may be elision." Donald Justice† adds: "This applies also to *l* and *n* and perhaps may be extended to *m.*" Examples:

   mur*muring;* pill*ar of* State; invisi*ble else;* rea*son has;* i*ron ore;* begot*ten, and.*

Further, according to Justice, "Final *m* and *n* are very frequently not counted anyhow, as in *chasm* or *heaven*. The words *evil* and *spirit* have also been frequently taken in English verse to have but one syllable. In contrast, *fire*

Milton's Prosody by Robert Bridges, Oxford: Oxford University Press, 1893.

†Examples and quotations taken from *Of Prosody* by Donald Justice, Iowa City, Iowa, 1960.

often is counted as two, *e.g.* Other characteristic words illustrating semi-vowel elision: suf*f*ering, endea*v*oring, gen*e*ral, se*v*eral, des*p*erate, am*o*rous, conqu*e*ror, po*p*ular, grove*l*ing, bu*s*iness, hard*e*ning, lumi*n*ous, o*p*ening.

"Elision in most of these words is optional; that is, the word need not be elided each time it occurs, even if it occurs twice in the same line."

MISCELLANEOUS DEVICES for rhythmic variation:

1. A perfect metrical line of verse is called an *acatalectic* line; the noun is *acatalexis*.

   a. By *dropping* a syllable at the *end* of the line, the line is made *catalectic;* the noun is *catalexis*.

   b. By *adding* a syllable at the *end* of the line, the line is made *hypercatalectic;* the noun is *hypercatalexis*.

   c. By *dropping* unaccented syllables from the *beginning* of the line, the line is made *acephalous;* the noun is *acephalexis*.

   d. By *adding* unaccented syllables to the *beginning* of the line, the line is made *anacrustic;* the noun is *anacrusis*.

The similarity and dissimilarity of sounds also are important to the poet:

TRUE RHYME consists of the *identical* sounds, in two or more words, of an *accented vowel* together with *all sounds following* that vowel while the *consonantal* sounds immediately *preceding* the vowel *differ* in each word. Thus, *b*ite, *tr*ite, *sl*eight, *n*ight, and de*l*ight are true rhymes.

FALSE RHYME has to do with the *identical* sound of the *consonant* or consonants immediately *preceding* the accented vowel, plus the vowels' subsequent sounds in two or more words. Thus, *c*yst, in*s*ist, per*s*ist, and solip*s*ist are false rhymes.

OFF-RHYME (slant rhyme) substitutes *similarity* of sound for identity of sound. Thus, bri*dge*, he*dge*, gou*ge*, enra*ge*, and even rou*ge* are slant rhymes. In effect, all vowels and vowel sounds (including diphthongs) are considered to be interchangeable, as are certain consonantal sounds that are related, such as the soft *g* in *gouge* and *enrage*, the harder *dg* in *bridge* and *hedge*, and the *zh* sound in *rouge* above.

ANALYZED RHYME is described by Edward Davison* thus: One "takes two such words as *soon* and *hide* but separates the vowel from the consonantal sounds before looking for his rhymes. The *oo* of *soon* is united with the *d* of *hide;* and the *i* of *hide* with the *h* of *soon*. This simple analysis produces the [four] rhyming sounds

oon	ine
ide	ood

as a basis for new sets of words. Thus, by means of analyzed rhyme an absolute sound relationship can be established among [four] words that have hitherto seemed alien to each other." A set of such words utilizing the sounds named above might be *croon*, *guide*, *line*, and *food*.

WRENCHED RHYME has to do with treating groups of words as though they were single words, thus: *sat on it* and *fat on it*.

A MASCULINE ENDING is a terminal measure that ends on an *accented* syllable. MASCULINE RHYME is thus the rhyming of two lines of verse with masculine endings. Also see *rising rhythms* in the section dealing with SAPPHICS.

A FEMININE ENDING is a terminal measure which ends on an *unaccented* syllable. FEMININE RHYME is thus the rhyming of two lines of verse with feminine endings. See also *falling rhythms* in the section on SAPPHICS.

LIGHT RHYME is the rhyming of one line of verse having a masculine ending with another line of verse having a feminine ending.

INTERNAL RHYME has to do with the ending of one line rhyming with a word buried in its own interior, usually the syllable before a caesura.

HEAD RHYME finds the syllables at the *beginnings* of lines rhyming.

LINKED RHYME has the *final* syllable(s) of a line rhyming with the *first* syllable(s) of the following line.

INTERLACED RHYME has a rhyme in the *middle* of the line

Some Modern Poets by Edward Lewis Davison, New York: Harper and Brothers, 1928.

which rhymes with a word also in the *middle* of a preceding or following line.

CROSS-RHYME has an end sound rhyming with a word buried in a preceding or following line.

AMPHISBAENIC RHYME is "backward" rhyme: *belated–detail; stop–pots; pets–*in*step.*

In APOCOPATED RHYME one or more syllables is dropped from the ending of *one* of a pair of rhyming words: chaingang–rain/; sing/–kingpin, etc.

In EYE RHYME words are spelled similarly but pronounced differently: *flies–homilies*, for instance.

SINGLE RHYMES are words of one syllable that rhyme; DOUBLE RHYMES are words of two syllables that rhyme; TRIPLE RHYMES have three syllables, and so forth.

ASSONANCE has to do with preserving identical accented *vowel* sounds but dispensing with identical consonant sounds. Thus, b*a*t, c*a*tch, g*a*p, m*a*d, l*a*ck, d*a*bble, and *a*nagr*a*m constitute an assonantal series. Usually assonance is used internally and in addition to rhyme when rhyme is present.

CONSONANCE is a synonym for OFF-RHYME (slant rhyme, near rhyme, etc.). The verb is CONSONATE.

ALLITERATION has to do with the repetition of initial stressed sounds, usually consonants. Thus, *t*rue, *t*utor, *t*ingle, *t*ips, *t*om-tom and *t*itillation comprise an alliterative sequence.

Euphony and *dissonance* have to do with quality of sounds, and EUPHONY means a *mingling of pleasant sounds*. Certain syllabic sounds have traditionally been adjudged to be either "pleasant" or "unpleasant." Thus, DISSONANCE means a *mingling of unpleasant sounds*, primarily hard consonants, while *euphonious* sounds would include all vowels and certain consonants, including *l*, *s*, *r*, *m*, soft *c*, and so forth. A CACOPHONY is a harsh or unpleasant mingling of sounds, both euphonious and dissonant.

Finally, REPETITION has to do with the formal re-use of words or lines of a poem. A REPETON is a whole line of verse that is formally repeated *one* other time elsewhere in the poem. A REPETEND is a line that appears more than once, but at random, unlike the REFRAIN, which is a phrase or line of verse that is formally repeated *at intervals* elsewhere in the poem. The difference between a refrain and a *burden* is that the latter is a stanza (a couplet or larger) that is repeated at intervals.

In these first chapters on metrics and sonics we have covered certain formal devices with which the poet may manipulate the *sounds* of the language in his ordering process. However, though poems may be, and have been, written utilizing only the sonic attributes of words, the poet will usually want his poem to mean something as well as be something. Therefore, in the next chapter we will talk about ways in which language may be intensified or heightened in order to achieve its fullest effects.

Chapter Three
Some Notes on Tropes

The dictionary defines *trope* as, "The use of a word or expression in a figurative sense: FIGURE OF SPEECH." Thus, a trope has to do with *figurative language*. All tropes are descriptive in nature, but not all descriptions are tropes. "One picture is worth a thousand words," the saying goes, but the poet knows that if he gets the right combination of words they may be better than a picture by a lot. Tropes are devices for intensifying descriptions. A description of a bird might be something like this: "A bird is a feathered animal having two four-clawed feet; two wings, with which most species fly; and a beak. It builds nests and hatches its young from eggs. Many birds eat insects or seeds, though some species prey on small game, carrion, or fish. . . ." A trope, however, might point out that "A bird is a live arrow."

This particular kind of trope is a METAPHOR: the *equation* of one thing with another, seemingly *unrelated* thing; yet both have at least one point in common, though that point may not be recognized easily. A SIMILE is sometimes called a "weaker metaphor"—it uses the words *like* or *as:* "A bird is *like* a live arrow."

A PUN is a play on words: two words sound alike, or nearly alike, and both meanings of the sound are used simultaneously for humorous effect, as in Hilaire Belloc's famous couplet,

> "When I am dead, I hope it may be said:
> 'His sins were scarlet, but his books were read.' "

A CONCEIT is an extended metaphor, simile, or pun, or a combination of all three; the poet extends and expands his orginal trope throughout the body of a whole poem, or a section of a poem. Poetry that does this is usually called, in the twentieth century, *metaphysical* poetry. Other elements that metaphysical poetry may utilize are irony, paradox, and wit in all its forms.

IRONY has to do with saying something, but actually meaning its opposite. For instance, in talking about a fat woman one might say, "She's a *great* girl." Here the ironical remark is also a pun.

A PARADOX is a statement that contains a contradiction that is nevertheless true, or a statement that is contrary to commonly held belief: "Freedom is the prison of rebellion," for instance, or "Winter is the Spring of contemplation."

An OXYMORON is a phrase that combines terms that are paradoxical: "sweet bitterness," "terrible beauty," etc.

All words have primary meanings, and these are called DENOTATIONS or denotative meanings. But most words also have, in certain contexts, secondary meanings, or CONNOTATIONS, and often the poet will want to "orchestrate" his poem by having both primary and secondary meanings operating simultaneously. Thus, *heart* means denotatively, "An organ of the body that pumps blood." But it can also refer to *courage*, or *love*, or to *essence*, as in the statement, "He is pure of heart." The poet, if he wishes to use the word's denotative meaning and *some* of its connotative meanings, must build a context in which those meanings can operate, but not those that he wishes to exclude. For instance, "His heart beat strongly in battle" includes the word's denotation, and its connotation *courage*, but excludes the other connotations.

There are other ways of describing, however. The most common method is, of course, by using a noun or verb plus modifiers. Some nouns are abstract. An ABSTRACTION is a nonspecificity. Such a word as *soul*, for example, may mean a number of things to various people. Other nouns are concrete; for instance, "well" may mean a hole driven into the ground for the purpose of providing water. The poet may make abstractions concrete by providing them with a context that makes them analogous to something concrete: "My soul is a dark, dry well." Such a concretion is an image.

An IMAGE, in the poetic sense, is a word picture. As you may have noted, we are now back where we started from—in a sense, all tropes are word pictures, or at least DE-

SCRIPTIONS: representations of things, feelings, actions, desires, and so forth, in language. There are a number of other ways of describing or intensifying:

A SYMBOL is some sign that represents something else. Thus, a white whale, in a specific context, might represent the enigma of existence.

An EMBLEM might be defined as a commonly held symbol —a crucifix stands for Christianity.

ALLEGORY is a method of telling a story on one level, but meaning something more general and symbolic regarding the human condition. Thus, the story of "The Ugly Duckling" is an allegory whose moral is, perhaps, that "beauty is in the eye of the beholder," or "everything turns out for the best."

PERSONIFICATION gives, on the other hand, human qualities to nonhuman things. As an example, Keats in his ode "To Autumn" addresses the season as though it were a person and says, "Who hath not seen thee oft amid thy store?/Sometimes whoever seeks abroad may find/Thee sitting careless on a granary floor,/Thy hair soft lifted by the winnowing wind; ... "

These lines also exhibit the rhetorical technique of APOSTROPHE or direct address. The poet in his poem addresses an absent or a (usually) personified thing or abstraction.

SYNESTHESIA is talking about one of the senses in terms of another: "The morning smelled blue," "I could taste her sweet whispers," and so forth.

ONOMATOPOEIA is a method of describing something by means of sonic and rhythmical devices, making the *sound* of the language imitate the thing, i.e., "The seashore roared from the seashell's folds."

APOSIOPESIS is a way of emphasizing a word by deleting it, but making that word obvious in a context—for instance, in a couplet such as, "All men who make passes/Are nothing but ..." the deleted word is obvious. Similarly, a word may be emphasized by changing it to another word: "All men who make passes/Are nothing but ... donkeys."

An ALLUSION in a poem is an indirect or implied reference

to something outside the poem, or something that is not organically a part of the poem, i.e., "He came, *like Rome*, to see, and stayed to conquer."

METONYMY is description by means of a word related to that which is to be described rather than by naming the thing itself: "The *flag* will find a way to win" instead of "the *country*" or "the *government*."

SYNECHDOCHE, similar to metonymy, substitutes a part for the whole: "He was a farm *hand*" rather than "farm *worker*."

HYPERBOLE is calculated exaggeration: "Her eyes were as big as saucers."

LITOTES, the reverse of hyperbole, is studied unterstatement: "Her eyes were eyes, and they were open."

A PERIPHRASIS is a way of saying something in a more grandiose or roundabout way than is usual: "She was taken to the bosom of her fathers," for instance, instead of "she died."

An ELLIPSIS, conversely, is a way of saying something in a starker manner than is usual: "I love darkness" instead of "I am in love with darkness."

In conclusion, we ought to note the term AMBIGUITY. William Empson, in his book entitled *Seven Types of Ambiguity*,* has abstracted seven ways in which ambiguity may enhance (or, to return to an earlier suggestion, *orchestrate*) poetry. Mr. Empson describes these ambiguities thus:

1) "First type ambiguities arise when a detail is effective in several ways at once, e.g., by comparisons with several points of likeness, antitheses with several points of difference, 'comparative' adjectives, subdued metaphors, and extra meanings suggested by rhythm."

2) " . . . two or more alternative meanings are fully resolved into one."

3) " . . . two apparently unconnected meanings are given simultaneously."

---

*Published in the U.S. by New Directions, Inc., and by Meridian Books in 1955.

4) " . . . the alternative meanings combine to make clear a complicated state of mind in the author."

5) " . . . a fortunate confusion, as when the author is discovering his idea in the act of writing . . . or not holding it all at once."

6) " . . . what is said is contradictory or irrelevant and the reader is forced to invent interpretations."

7) " . . . full contradiction, marking a division in the author's mind."

The reader is referred to the book for more complete information and examples.

So much for the techniques of versification. It remains now for you to try your skills within some kind of construct. The remainder of *The Book of Forms* is the most complete assemblage of traditional verse forms ever collected in America, or perhaps anywhere, in one volume. Some of the forms are simple, some extremely complex. They will provide you with ample devices for testing your mastery of the language, and your growth as a *maker*.

Chapter Four
The Book of Forms

FORM-FINDER

In order to identify the form of a poem you have been reading, do the following *first;* a) determine its *meter;* b) determine its *rhyme scheme;* c) count the lines in *one stanza* (if you are looking for a stanza form) *or* the number of lines in the whole poem (if you are looking for a poem form).

When you have done these things, d) look under the appropriate heading of the Form-Finder: if the form is irregular, look under *Irregular Forms;* if the form is regular, look under *Regular Forms,* then under the appropriate sub-heading (One-Line Forms through Two-Hundred-Line Forms). If you think the form is regular, but you cannot find it listed, then check the Irregular Forms.

Under these various headings you will find lists of forms that you may look up in the body of Chapter Four, which you should compare with your poem until you find the form in which your poem is written.

REGULAR FORMS:

One-Line Forms
adonic (see *Sapphics*)
Alexandrine (see *Poulter's measure*)
Anglo-Saxon prosody
blank verse
choriambics
cyhydedd naw ban
classical hexameter (see *elegiacs*)
    classical pentameter
fourteener (see *Poulter's measure*)

32

free verse
   Nasher
   antithetical parallel
   climactic parallel
   synonymous parallel
   synthetic parallel
hendecasyllabics
heroic line (see *heroics*)
Hudibrastics (see *satirics*)
mote
rhupunt
Sapphic line (see *Sapphics*)
septenary (see *Poulter's measure*)
tawddgyrch cadwynog (see *rhupunt*)

Two-Line Forms
carol texte
couplet
   cyhydedd fer
   cywydd deuair fyrion
   cywydd deuair hirion
   qasida
   short couplet
   split couplet
elegiacs
heroic couplet (see *heroics*)
Hudibrastics (see *satirics*)
Poulter's measure
primer couplet (see *didactics*)
tanka couplet (see *tanka*)

Three-Line Forms
tercet
   enclosed tercet
   haiku
   Sicilian tercet
terza rima
triplet
   enclosed triplet

    englyn milwr
    englyn penfyr
    Sicilian triplet
triversen stanza

Four-Line Forms
ae freislighe
alcaics
awdl gywydd
ballad stanza
ballade envoy
    ballade à double refrain envoy
byr a thoddaid
carol stanza
casbairdne
common measure
    hymnal stanza
    long hymnal stanza
    long measure
    short hymnal stanza
    short measure
deibhidhe
englyn cyrch (see *englyns*)
    englyn lleddfbroest
    englyn proest dalgron
    englyn proest gadwynog
    englyn unodl crwca
    englyn unodl union
glose texte
gwawdodyn
heroic stanza (see *heroics*)
kyrielle
pantoum
quatrain
    envelope stanza
    Italian quatrain
    redondilla
    Sicilian quatrain

rannaigheacht ghairid (see *rannaigheachts*)
  deachnadh mór
  randaigecht chetharchubaid
  rannaigheacht bheag
  rannaigheacht mhór
rionnaird tri n-ard
rispetto stanza
rubai
Sapphics
séadna
  séadna mór
sneadhbhairdne
toddaid
wheel (see *bob and wheel*)

Five-Line Forms
ballade suprême envoy
bob and wheel
chant royal envoy
cinquain
limerick
  madsong stanza
quintet
  quintilla
  Sicilian quintet
tanka

Six-Line Forms
clogyrnach
cywydd llosgyrnog
gwawdodyn hir (see *gwawdodyn*)
hir a thoddaid
rime couée
  standard habbie
sestet
  heroic sestet
  Italian sestet
  sextilla
  Sicilian sestet

short particular measure (see *common measure*)
stave
  couplet envelope

Seven-Line Forms
rime royal
rondelet
septet
  Sicilian septet

Eight-Line Forms
ballade stanza
  ballade à double refrain stanza
  double ballade stanza
  huitain
common octave (see *common measure*)
  hymnal octave
  long hymnal octave
  long octave
  short hymnal octave
  short octave
cyhydedd hir
cyrch a chuta
lai nouveau (see *lai*)
octave
  Italian octave
  Sicilian octave
  strambotto
madrigal
ottava rima
rispetto
  heroic octave
  heroic rispetto
triolet

Nine-Line Forms
lai
  virelai
Ronsardian ode stanza
Spenserian stanza

triad (see *tercet*)

Ten-Line Forms
ballade suprême stanza
   dizain
   double ballade suprême stanza
English ode stanza (see *ode*)
glose stanza
madrigal

Eleven-Line Forms
chant royal stanza
madrigal
roundel

Twelve-Line Forms
Pearline stanza
rondeau prime (see *rondeau*)

Thirteen-Line Forms
madrigal
rondel

Fourteen-Line Forms

bref double
   quatorzain
rondel prime (see *rondel*)
sonetto rispetto (see *rispetto*)
sonnet
   English sonnet
   Italian sonnet
   Spenserian sonnet
terza rima sonnet (see *terza rima*)

Fifteen-Line Forms
rondeau

Eighteen-Line Forms
heroic sonnet (see *sonnet*)
triversen

Nineteen-Line Forms
terzanelle
villanelle

Twenty-Line Forms
caudated sonnet (see *sonnet*)

Twenty-Five-Line Forms
rondeau redoublé (see *rondeau*)

Twenty-Eight-Line Forms
ballade
    ballade à double refrain

Thirty-Line Forms
English ode (see *ode*)

Thirty-Five-Line Forms
ballade suprême (see *ballade*)

Thirty-Nine-Line Forms
sestina

Forty-Eight-Line Forms
double ballade (see *ballade*)

Sixty-Line Forms
chant royal
double ballade suprême (see *ballade*)

Ninety-Eight-Line Forms
crown of sonnets (see *sonnet*)

Two-Hundred-Line Forms
Qasida

Two-Hundred-Ten-Line Forms
sonnet redoublé (see *sonnet*)

IRREGULAR FORMS:

acrostic
    double acrostic
ballad

didactics
  epistle
  georgics
  riddle

dramatics
  dialogue
  eclogue
  monologue
  soliloquy
droighneach

free verse
  polyphonic prose
  prose poem

lyrics
  alba (aubade)
  anacreontics
  canso (canzo, canzone)
  canticle
  carol
  chant
  chantey
  dithyramb
  elegy (dirge, monody, threnody)
  epithalamion
  lay
  madrigal
  madsong
  nursery rhyme
  pastoral (idyl)
  pastoral elegy
  prothalamion
  riddle
  romance
  roundelay
  rune
  serenade
  sirvente

ode
  homostrophic ode
  irregular (Cowleyan) ode
  Pindaric ode
palinode
satirics
  epigram
  epitaph
  Skeltonics
spatials (calligramme, hieroglyphic verse, shaped stanza)
  concrete verse

ACROSTIC

May be in any of the meters or in any form. What is of primary importance is that the first letters of all lines, when read downward, spell out a word or a phrase, usually a name. The DOUBLE ACROSTIC repeats this feat with the last letters of the lines as well.

A typical scheme:

lines:	first letter of first word:
1.	J-
2.	O-
3.	H-
4.	N-
5.	D-
6.	O-
7.	E-

Note that separate words usually form separate stanzas.

A scheme for a double acrostic:

lines:	first and last letters:	
1.	E-	-e
2.	V-	-v
3.	E-	-e
4.	R-	-r
5.	Y-	-y
6.	M-	-m
7.	A-	-a
8.	N-	-n
9.	I-	-i
10.	N-	-n
11.	L-	-l
12.	O-	-o
13.	V-	-v
14.	E-	-e

See also the RUNE in the LYRICS section.

AE FREISLIGHE

Irish. Syllabic.

Since this is the first of the Celtic forms to be encountered in *The Book of Forms*, perhaps a note is in order. Almost all of the Irish and Welsh forms are very complex systems of rhyme, alliteration, and consonance (called, collectively, *cynghanedd*). For the practical purpose of versification in English it should be understood that the systems are almost impossible to reproduce accurately in our language. Therefore, perhaps it would be as well for the poet attempting these forms to pay most attention only to the rhyme scheme and syllabification. Thus, ae freislighe simplified would be a QUATRAIN stanza of seven-syllable lines. Lines *one* and *three* rhyme in triple rhymes; lines *two* and *four* rhyme in double rhymes.

The *poem* (not the stanza) should end with the same first syllable, word, or line with which it begins. The technical term for this ending is *dúnadh*, and it occurs in all the Gaelic forms.

The diagram:

lines:	syllables and rhymes:
1.	x x x x x x a
2.	x x x x x x b
3.	x x x x x x a
4.	x x x x x x b

This form should not be confused with the SICILIAN QUATRAIN, which has a similar rhyme scheme.

ALCAICS

Greek. Accentual-syllabic. Unrhymed. A QUATRAIN stanza. The first two lines consist of an acephalous iamb, two trochees, and two dactyls, in that order; the third line consists of an acephalous iamb and four trochees, in that order; the fourth line is made of two dactyls followed by two trochees.

The pattern:

lines:	*meters:*				
1.	x́	x́x	x́x	x́xx	x́xx
2.	x́	x́x	x́x	x́xx	x́xx
3.	x́	x́x	x́x	x́x	x́x
4.	x́xx	x́xx	x́x	x́x	

Accentual. A LINE utilizing alliteration and stress. It is composed of two half-lines separated by a *caesura* or rhythmic pause. Each half-line is called a *hemistich* and owns two accented syllables. Thus, there are *four accents to the full line*. There may be *any number of unaccented syllables* in a line.

The *initial sounds* of the first three *accented syllables* are alliterated. Though exactly the same *consonant* sounds must be alliterated, any *vowel* may "alliterate" with any other vowel: actually, what is being alliterated in the latter case is the *absence* of consonants.

Although it is *not a requirement* of the form, the alliteration *may* at times be continued into the fourth accented syllable. Also, sometimes the *fourth* accented syllable of a line becomes the alliteration in the following line.

Here is a diagram of some possible lines of Anglo-Saxon prosody:

lines:	words, syllables, alliterations, accents, caesuras:
1.	xx áxx x áx · á xxxx b́x x
2.	ćxxx xxx ć · ćx x d́xx
3.	d́x d́xx · d́ xxx d́
4.	xx xxx é x éx · x éxx f́x
5.	etcetera.

See also the PEARLINE STANZA and *sprung rhythm*. For a form sometimes associated with Anglo-Saxon prosody, see the BOB AND WHEEL.

AWDL GYWYDD

Welsh. Syllabic. A QUATRAIN stanza of seven-syllable lines. Lines *two* and *four* rhyme; lines one and three *cross-rhyme into* the third, fourth, *or* fifth *syllable* of lines two and four.

Here is a possible scheme for three stanzas of awdl gywydd:

lines:	*syllables and rhymes:*						
1.	x	x	x	x	x	x	a
2.	x	x	*a*	*x*	*x*	x	b
3.	x	x	x	x	x	x	c
4.	x	x	*x*	*x*	*c*	x	b
5.	x	x	x	x	x	x	d
6.	x	x	*x*	*d*	*x*	x	e
7.	x	x	x	x	x	x	f
8.	x	x	*x*	*f*	*x*	x	e
9.	x	x	x	x	x	x	g
10.	x	x	*x*	*x*	*g*	x	h
11.	x	x	x	x	x	x	i
12.	x	x	*x*	*i*	*x*	x	h

13.   etcetera.

BALLAD

Universal in the western world. Usually accentual-syllabic. The BALLAD STANZA is often $a^4b^3c^4b^3$: here the letters stand for rhymes, the numbers stand for the number of metrical feet to a line. The ballad is not, however, a fixed form. It may be written in any meter. Often it is rhymed, and *internal rhyme* is sometimes used. There is no fixed stanza or line length, and it often has a *refrain* or *burden*. Meant to be sung, the ballad may be defined as a *lyrical* verse *narrative*, for ballads tell stories.

Here is a possible pattern for one loose anapestic ballad stanza with internal rhymes and refrain:

lines:	meters, rhymes, refrain:
1.	xxx́ xá xxx́ xxá
2.	xx́ xxx́ xb́
3.	xxx́ xxć xxx́ xxć
4.	xxx́ xxx́ xB́—*refrain*

For related forms see COMMON MEASURE. For other narrative forms see the LAY and ROMANCE in the section on LYRICS, the EPIC in the section on HEROICS, and the FABLIAU in the section titled VERSE NARRATIVES.

A distinction is often made between the FOLK BALLAD, which is traditional and anonymous, and the LITERARY BALLAD, which is a composition by a known author. The former often manifests a phenomenon called "leaping and lingering," which means that the folk ballad skips from high point to high point, ignoring details of the narrative, whereas the literary ballad develops the whole narrative, including details and climaxes. For more information concerning the metric of the ballad, see *dipodics*.

BALLADE

A French form. Syllabic. Lines may be of any length, but are usually of eight or ten syllables. Twenty-eight lines divided in three OCTAVE stanzas and one QUATRAIN half-stanza, which is called the *envoi* or *envoy*. The ballade turns on three rhymes and is built on a *refrain*, which appears as the last line of each stanza and of the envoy.

Here is the scheme for the first stanza:

lines:	rhymes:
1.	a
2.	b
3.	a
4.	b
5.	b
6.	c
7.	b
8.	C—*refrain*

The second stanza (lines nine through sixteen) and the third stanza (lines seventeen through twenty-four) are exactly the same. Here is the scheme for the envoy:

25.	b
26.	c
27.	b
28.	C—*refrain*

Note well: there are only *three rhymes in the whole poem*, and no rhyme or rhyme word should be repeated.

The BALLADE SUPRÊME has thirty-five lines: three ten-line stanzas rhyming ababbccdcD with an envoy of five lines rhyming ccdcD. The refrain appears as the last line of each stanza and of the envoy. Note that this form has four rhymes.

The DOUBLE BALLADE and the DOUBLE BALLADE SUPRÊME have six stanzas of either eight or ten lines respectively and follow the rhyme schemes of the ballade and the ballade suprême. An envoy is *optional;* if one is used, it is the same as in the ballade and ballade suprême. The refrain appears as the last line of each stanza and of the envoy.

The BALLADE À DOUBLE REFRAIN has three eight-line stanzas rhyming abaBbcbC with an envoy of four lines rhyming bBcC. It has two refrains. The first refrain appears as lines four, twelve, twenty, and twenty-six; the second refrain appears as lines eight, sixteen, twenty-four, and twenty-eight.

The CHANT ROYAL, a member of the ballade family, is listed separately.

The HUITAIN is a complete poem composed of one ballade stanza (*ababbcbc*); Huitains used as stanzas are called MONK'S TALE STANZA. The DIZAIN is a complete poem composed of one ballade suprême stanza (*ababbccdcd*). The lines are either eight or ten syllables in length for both forms (in English metrics, iambic tetrameter or pentameter).

Note that the addition of an *Alexandrine* line to the iambic pentameter huitain, to form a final couplet, will result in one SPENSERIAN STANZA: *ababbcbcc*[6].

BLANK VERSE

Accentual-syllabic. Strictly speaking, blank verse is a LINE of any unrhymed, *metered* verse. However, it is more commonly understood to mean *unrhymed iambic pentameter verse*. Note that *free verse is not blank verse;* blank verse is *metered*, free verse is not.

line: *meters:*
  1.   xx́ xx́ xx́ xx́ xx́

See also HEROICS.

BOB AND WHEEL

The "bob and wheel" is an English *accentual-syllabic* QUINTET *stanza* that is sometimes found in association with *accentual* poems. Specifically, it is a *metrical tail* on a stanza of Anglo-Saxon prosody.

The final line of the *accentual stanza* proper is usually a run-on line that is continued by the BOB: a line of verse composed of one *or* two verse feet—sometimes of only one accented syllable. The bob itself may be a run-on line that is continued and completed by the WHEEL: four lines, each of which consists of *three* verse feet.

The *bob* rhymes with lines *two* and *four* of the wheel; lines *one* and *three* of the wheel rhyme with each other.

This is the structure of the entire bob and wheel:

lines:	*meters and rhymes:*		
1.	... xx	xá	
2.	xx́	xx́	xb́
3.	xx́	xx́	xá
4.	xx́	xx́	xb́
5.	xx́	xx́	xá

For the form with which it is most commonly associated, see ANGLO-SAXON PROSODY.

BREF DOUBLE

French. Syllabic. Lines may be of any length. Fourteen lines arranged in three QUATRAIN stanzas and a concluding COUPLET. There are only three rhymes in the poem, but not every line is rhymed. The *a* rhyme appears twice somewhere within the three quatrains and once in the couplet. The *b* rhyme does likewise. The *c* rhyme ends each quatrain. A possible scheme:

lines:	rhymes:
1.	a
2.	x—*no rhyme*
3.	b
4.	c
5.	x—*no rhyme*
6.	b
7.	x—*no rhyme*
8.	c
9.	x—*no rhyme*
10.	a
11.	x—*no rhyme*
12.	c
13.	a
14.	b

This form is thought to be an ancestor of the SONNET. Actually, the bref double is a QUATORZAIN: any stanza or poem of fourteen lines *other than* a sonnet. Other quatorzains with set forms are the SONETTO RISPETTO and the TERZA RIMA sonnet.

BYR A THODDAID

Welsh. Syllabic. This QUATRAIN *stanza* combines a COUPLET consisting of eight syllables per line with another COUPLET consisting of ten syllables in the *first* line and six syllables in the *second* line. In the *ten-syllable line* the *main rhyme* is found *before* the end of the line, and the syllables that *follow* the main rhyme in the ten-syllable line must be *linked* by means of alliteration, assonance, or *secondary rhyme* with the *early syllables* of the first part of the *six-syllable* line. In the quatrain either couplet may follow the other.

Note that in this scheme primary or *main rhymes are in capital letters;* alliteration, assonances, or *secondary rhymes are indicated by means of small letters:*

lines:	syllables and rhymes:
1.	x x x x x x x A
2.	x x x x x x x A
3.	x x x x x x x B *x c*
4.	*x c x* x x B
5.	x x x x x x D *x x e*
6.	*e x x* x x D
7.	x x x x x x x F
8.	x x x x x x x F
9.	etcetera.

CAROL

French and English. Generally speaking, a carol is simply a "joyous hymn" (see p. 80). However, it originally had a more-or-less set form that consisted of a two-line *burden* or *texte* COUPLET rhyming A^1A^2, and any number of QUATRAIN stanzas rhyming *bbba*. The last lines of these stanzas rhymed with the burden, or they echoed or repeated one or the other of the burden lines. Usually the meter was short, trimeter or tetrameter; no set verse foot. The whole burden might be repeated at intervals.

A possible scheme:

lines:	meters, rhymes, refrains:
1.	xx́ xx́ xx́ xÁ¹ ⎫ TEXTE (burden)
2.	xx́ xx́ xx́ xÁ² ⎭
3.	xx́ xx́ xx́ xb́
4.	xx́ xx́ xx́ xb́
5.	xx́ xx́ xx́ xb́
6.	xx́ xx́ xx́ xá or A¹ or A²
7.	xx́ xx́ xx́ xć
8.	xx́ xx́ xx́ xć
9.	xx́ xx́ xx́ xć
10.	xx́ xx́ xx́ xá or A¹ or A²
11.	xx́ xx́ xx́ xÁ¹
12.	xx́ xx́ xx́ xÁ²
13.	etcetera.

For other forms that use a *texte*, see the GLOSE, the RONDEAU REDOUBLÉ, and the SONNET REDOUBLÉ.

CASBAIRDNE

Irish. Syllabic. A QUATRAIN *stanza* of heptasyllabic lines with trisyllabic endings. Lines *two* and *four* rhyme, and lines *one* and *three* consonate (not rhyme) with them. There are at least two *cross-rhymes* in each couplet; in the first couplet these need *not* be exact. There is alliteration as in RAN-NAIGHEACHT MHÓR, the final syllable of line *four* alliterating with the *preceding stressed word*.

The *poem* (not the stanza) ends with the same first syllable, word, or line with which it begins.

A simplified version:

lines:	syllables and rhymes:

1.	x	x	b	x	x	x	a
2.	x	a	x	x	x	x	b
3.	x	x	x	b	x	x	c
4.	x	x	c	x	x	x	d

1. x x b x x̲ x̲ a̲
2. x a x x x̲ x̲ b̲ —*consonate*
3. x x x b x̲ x̲ c̲
4. x x c x x̲ x̲ d̲ —*consonate*

54

CHANT ROYAL

A French form. Syllabic. Lines may be of any length. Sixty lines divided into five eleven-line stanzas and one five-line *envoy*. The chant royal turns on five rhymes and is built on a *refrain*. Strictly speaking, it is a form of the BALLADE.

This is the scheme of *all* stanzas:

lines:	rhymes:
1.	a
2.	b
3.	a
4.	b
5.	c
6.	c
7.	d
8.	d
9.	e
10.	d
11.	E—*refrain*

and this is the scheme of the *envoy:*

56.	d
57.	d
58.	e
59.	d
60.	E—*refrain*

CHORIAMBICS

Greek. Accentual-syllabic. A LINE consisting, in this order, of two trochees, an iamb, a trochee, an iamb, a trochee, and two iambs. Unrhymed. Poems may consist of any number of lines.

Scheme for one line:

line: *meters:*
1.   x́x   x́x   xx́   x́x   xx́   x́x   xx́   xx́

CINQUAIN

An American form. Syllabic or accentual-syllabic. Five lines long, the lines consist of two, four, six, eight, and two syllables respectively. It is unrhymed, a set form of the QUINTET.

Originally the poem was written in iambs: one iambic foot in the first line, two in the second, three in the third, four in the fourth, and one in the fifth line.

Here is the scheme in syllabics:

lines: *syllables:*
1.   x x
2.   x x x x
3.   x x x x x x
4.   x x x x x x x x
5.   x x

For similar forms see the HAIKU in the section dealing with the TERCET, and the TANKA.

CLOGYRNACH

A Welsh form. Syllabic. A SESTET *stanza* having lines with counts of eight, eight, five, five, three, and three syllables respectively. The two three-syllable lines may, if desired, be written as one six-syllable line. The rhyme scheme is *aabbba*.

A diagram of one stanza of clogyrnach is as follows:

lines:	syllables and rhymes:
1.	x x x x x x x x a
2.	x x x x x x x x a
3.	x x x x b
4.	x x x x b
5.	x x b
6.	x x a
7.	etcetera.

COMMON MEASURE

Accentual-syllabic. Rhymed. A QUATRAIN *stanza* written in strict iambics, unlike the BALLAD *stanza*, which is otherwise similar. The rhyme scheme is *abcb*. The *first* and *third* lines consist of four iambic feet; the *second* and *fourth* lines of three iambic feet. Thus, a simple scheme of the stanza might be written $a^4b^3c^4b^3$.

A complete scheme:

lines:	meters and rhymes:			
1.	xx́	xx́	xx́	xá
2.	xx́	xx́	xb́	
3.	xx́	xx́	xx́	xć
4.	xx́	xx́	xb́	

HYMNAL STANZA is the same except that it rhymes *abab*.

SHORT MEASURE, a form of common measure, appears thus: $a^3b^3c^4b^3$; SHORT HYMNAL STANZA is similar: $a^3b^3a^4b^3$. LONG MEASURE rhymes *abcb*, but all lines are iambic tetrameter, as are the lines in LONG HYMNAL STANZA, which rhymes *abab*.

All forms of common measure and hymnal stanza may be doubled to make OCTAVE stanzas. These are called COMMON OCTAVE, HYMNAL OCTAVE, SHORT OCTAVE, SHORT HYMNAL OCTAVE, LONG OCTAVE, and LONG HYMNAL OCTAVE.

SHORT PARTICULAR MEASURE is a SESTET *stanza* that has three iambic feet in lines *one*, *two*, *four*, and *five;* and four feet in lines *three* and *six*. It usually rhymes $a^3a^3b^4a^3a^3b^4$. For a reversal of this pattern see RIME COUÉE.

COUPLET

Any two lines, written as a unit. May be in any length and in any meter. Most couplets rhyme *aa*. There are several set forms.

The SHORT COUPLET is written in either *iambic* or *trochaic tetrameter*. The pattern in iambics:

lines:	meters and rhymes:
1.	xx́ xx́ xx́ xá
2.	xx́ xx́ xx́ xá

The SPLIT COUPLET is also accentual-syllabic. It consists of two lines, the *first* of which is written in *iambic pentameter* measures, the *second* in iambic dimeter:

1.	xx́ xx́ xx́ xx́ xá
2.	xx́ xá

There are three Welsh couplets, all of them syllabic.

CYHYDEDD FER is a rhymed couplet, of which each line contains eight syllables.

CYWYDD DEUAIR FYRION has each line containing four syllables, and it is rhymed.

CYWYDD DEUAIR HIRION is a light-rhyming couplet—that is, the first line is masculine, ending on a stressed or *accented syllable*, and the second line is feminine, ending on an unstressed or *unaccented syllable*, and the lines rhyme *aa*. A schematic for two couplets:

lines:	syllables, rhymes, accents:
1.	x́ x x́ x x́ x á
2.	x́ x x́ x x x́ a
3.	x́ x x́ x́ x x b́
4.	x x́ x x́ x x́ b

Note that each line of cywydd deuair hirion contains seven syllables, and that the accents need not be regular (metrical).

The QASĪDA, an Arabic form, consists of any number of couplets, up to one hundred, all turning on the same rhyme.

For other set forms of the couplet see the sections on DIDACTICS, FREE VERSE, HEROICS, and POULTER'S MEASURE.

CYHYDEDD HIR

Welsh. Syllabic. OCTAVE *stanzas* composed of two QUA-TRAINS each of whose four lines consist of five, five, five, and four, syllables respectively. Each quatrain may, if desired, be arranged as a single nineteen-syllable line. The five-syllable lines in each quatrain rhyme with one another; the four-syllable lines carry the *main rhyme*.

Strictly speaking, the stanzas need *not* be octave stanzas. Any number of quatrains may be used in a stanza and technically the meter will remain cyhydedd hir. However, within any stanza the short lines must carry the same rhyme.

Scheme of two octave stanzas:

lines:	syllables and rhymes:
1.	x x x x a
2.	x x x x a
3.	x x x x a
4.	x x x B
5.	x x x x c
6.	x x x x c
7.	x x x x c
8.	x x x B
9.	x x x x d
10.	x x x x d
11.	x x x x d
12.	x x x E
13.	x x x x f
14.	x x x x f
15.	x x x x f
16.	x x x E
17.	etcetera.

CYHYDEDD NAW BAN

Welsh. Syllabic. A LINE of nine syllables. It *must* rhyme with at least one other line of equal length to form a couplet. However, it may continue the rhyme throughout the stanza, which may be of any length, provided that all lines are equal in length.

The scheme for three lines:

lines:	syllables and rhymes:								
1.	x	x	x	x	x	x	x	x	a
2.	x	x	x	x	x	x	x	x	a
3.	x	x	x	x	x	x	x	x	a
4.	etcetera.								

This form should not be confused with the QASIDA.

CYRCH A CHUTA

Welsh. Syllabic. An OCTAVE *stanza* of six rhyming or slant-rhyming seven-syllable lines plus a couplet, the *second* line of which rhymes with the first six lines. The first line of the couplet (line seven) *cross-rhymes into* the third, fourth, or fifth syllable of line eight.

The scheme for one stanza:

lines:	syllables and rhymes:						
1.	x	x	x	x	x	x	a
2.	x	x	x	x	x	x	a
3.	x	x	x	x	x	x	a
4.	x	x	x	x	x	x	a
5.	x	x	x	x	x	x	a
6.	x	x	x	x	x	x	a
7.	x	x	x	x	x	x	b
8.	x	x	*x*	*b*	*x*	x	a
9.	etcetera.						

CYWYDD LLOSGYRNOG

A Welsh form. Syllabic. A SESTET *stanza*, the lines having respective syllable counts of eight, eight, seven, eight, eight, and seven syllables. Lines *one* and *two* rhyme, and cross-rhyme with the *middle* syllable of line *three*; lines *four* and *five* rhyme, and cross-rhyme with the *middle* syllable of line *six*; lines *three* and *six* rhyme with each other.

Here is the schematic for a stanza:

lines:	syllables and rhymes:
1.	x x x x x x x a
2.	x x x x x x x a
3.	x x x *a* x x b
4.	x x x x x x x c
5.	x x x x x x x c
6.	x x x *c* x x b
7.	etcetera.

This form should not be confused with RIME COUÉE, which has a similar rhyme scheme.

DEIBHIDHE

Irish. Syllabic. A QUATRAIN *stanza* light-rhyming in couplets. There is alliteration between two words in each line, the final word of line *four* alliterating with the preceding stressed word. There are at least two cross-rhymes between lines *three* and *four*. Each line has seven syllables.

The *poem* (not the stanza) ends with the same first syllable, word, or line with which it begins.

The diagram for one stanza:

lines:	syllables, rhymes; accented endings:
1.	x x x x x x x á
2.	x x x x x x́ a
3.	x b x x x x b́
4.	x x x b x x́ b

DIDACTICS

There are four didactic forms in English prosody.

The EPISTLE is a loose form. It is a letter to someone or to mankind in general, and it serves as a medium for hortatory instruction.

The PRIMER COUPLET, a set form, is a dipodic (two-verse-foot) couplet rhyming *aa*. Essentially, primer couplets are rhymed aphorisms.

A scheme for a primer couplet in iambs:

lines:	*meters and rhymes:*
1.	xx́ xá
2.	xx́ xá

The RIDDLE is a short lyric that poses a question, the answer to which lies hidden in hints.

GEORGICS are rhymed instructions or directions in the arts, sciences, or trades; versified handbooks.

DRAMATICS

There are three loose verse forms which can exist outside the drama proper.

A DIALOGUE is a conversation in verse among two or more characters.

The MONOLOGUE (or *dramatic monologue*, as it is sometimes called) is a verse speech by a single character. However, a listening audience is assumed, and the speaker addresses himself to his listeners (the reader or a silent character).

The SOLILOQUY is similar, but the speaker is assumed to be alone, and his speech consists of his private thoughts verbalized.

A fourth form is not, specifically speaking, a dramatic form. The ECLOGUE (or *bucolic*) is really a PASTORAL (see the section on LYRICS). However, it is cast in the form of a dialogue between two herdsmen or shepherds.

DROIGHNEACH

Irish. Syllabic. A loose *stanza* form. The single line may consist of from nine to thirteen syllables, and it *always* ends in a trisyllabic word. There is rhyme between lines *one* and *three*, *two* and *four*, etc. There are at least two cross-rhymes in each couplet. There is alliteration in each line—usually the final word of the line alliterates with the preceding stressed word, and it *always* does so in the *last* line of each stanza. Stanzas may consist of any number of quatrains.

The *poem* (not the stanza) ends with the same first syllable, word, or line with which it begins.

A possible scheme:

lines:	*syllables and rhymes:*
1.	x x b x x x x x̲ x̲ a
2.	x x x x a x x x̲ x̲ x b
3.	x x x x x b x̲ x̲ a
4.	x x x x a x x̲ x̲ b
5.	x x x x x d x x̲ x̲ c
6.	x x x c x x x x x̲ x̲ x̲ x d
7.	x x d x x x x x x̲ x̲ x̲ c
8.	x x x x c x x̲ x̲ d
9.	etcetera.

ELEGIACS

Greek. Accentual-syllabic. A COUPLET measure. The *first line* is a CLASSICAL HEXAMETER: the *first four* feet are either spondees or dactyls, the *fifth* foot is a dactyl, the *sixth* is a spondee.

The *second line* of the couplet is a CLASSICAL PENTAMETER, which consists, in this order, of *two* dactyls, a spondee, and *two* anapests. It may be rhymed or unrhymed.

A possible scheme:

lines:	*meters:*					
1.	x́xx	x́xx	x́xx	x́xx	x́xx	x́x́
2.	x́xx	x́xx	x́x́	xxx́	xxx́	

See also the ELEGY and PASTORAL ELEGY in the section on LYRICS.

Welsh. Syllabic. There are eight englyns. Six of them, those treated in this section, are QUATRAIN *stanzas.*

ENGLYN CYRCH has seven syllables in each line. Lines *one* and *two* and *four* turn on a single rhyme. Line *three* cross-rhymes *into* one of the three central syllables of line *four:*

lines:	syllables and rhymes:						
1.	x	x	x	x	x	x	a
2.	x	x	x	x	x	x	a
3.	x	x	x	x	x	x	b
4.	x	x	*x*	*x*	*b*	x	a
5.	etcetera.						

Each line of ENGLYN LLEDDFBROEST *diphthong-rhymes* with the others and has a count of seven syllables. In Welsh, the rhymes used were the four diphthongs *ae, oe, wy,* and *ei.* Since this is impossible to reproduce in English, any *similar diphthongs* may be substituted and may be considered to rhyme with one another. A one stanza schematic:

lines:	syllables and diphthong-rhymes:						
1.	x	x	x	x	x	x	oe
2.	x	x	x	x	x	x	wy
3.	x	x	x	x	x	x	ei
4.	x	x	x	x	x	x	ae
5.	etcetera.						

ENGLYN PROEST DALGRON has in each line a count of seven syllables. The lines *off-rhyme* on vowels or similar diphthongs. A possible scheme:

lines:	syllables and off-rhymes:						
1.	x	x	x	x	x	x	oi
2.	x	x	x	x	x	x	ay
3.	x	x	x	x	x	x	ou
4.	x	x	x	x	x	x	uy
5.	etcetera.						

In ENGLYN PROEST GADWYNOG each line has seven syllables. Lines *one* and *three* rhyme; lines *two* and *four* off-rhyme with lines *one* and *three* and with each other:

lines:	syllables, off-rhymes, and rimes:
1.	x x x x x x r
2.	x x x x x x or
3.	x x x x x x r
4.	x x x x x x or
5.	etcetera.

ENGLYN UNODL CRWCA has lines that have syllable counts of seven, seven, ten, and six respectively. Lines *one*, *two*, and *four* end with the *main* rhyme. In line *three* the main rhyme is followed by one, two, or three *syllables* that are *echoed* by assonance, alliteration, *or* secondary rhyme in the first part of the *fourth* line:

lines:	syllables and rhymes:
1.	x x x x x x A
2.	x x x x x x A
3.	x x x x x x A *x x b*
4.	*x b x* x x A
5.	etcetera.

ENGLYN UNODL UNION merely shifts the positions of the two couplets that make up englyn unodl crwca: lines *three* and *four* of the latter become lines *one* and *two*, and lines *one* and *two* become lines *three* and *four* of the englyn unodl union.

Two other englyns will be found in the section on TRIPLETS.

FREE VERSE

The term "free verse" is derived from the French *vers libre*, which Ezra Pound, Amy Lowell, and others began to popularize during the 'teens and 'twenties of this century, in the pages of Harriet Monroe's *Poetry* magazine and elsewhere. But as it is applied to English prosodies, the term is misleading, if not actually inapplicable.

As one may easily see, in looking through the forms of this book, the French prosodic system is syllabic, not accentual. The reason for this is that the French consider their language to be *without* stresses; thus, they are precluded from using any accentual or metrical (accentual-syllabic) system. It should be clear, then, that if the French refrain from writing lines that contain specific numbers of syllables, their verse is "free." However, this is *not* the case with verse written in English.

The English language is emphatically a stressed language —we can hear the cadences of our words. It has been said, in fact, that English is basically an iambic language. And we say, further, that any English-language poet, whether he be a "free verse" poet or otherwise, must have an "ear" . . . that is, an ear for cadences.

Therefore, it should be obvious that English poetry can never be "free" in the sense that French poetry may be *libre*. No matter what the English-speaking poet may do, his verse will be basically accentual (though he may use other systems *besides* accentuals). In fact, one might go so far as to point out that *most free verse poems in English are basically iambic, or mixtures of iambic and anapestic meters.*

Finally, it comes down to this: the term "free verse," as it is applied to poetry in English, is a misnomer that has clouded the issue for years. A term such as "random metrics," denoting a certain variation in lengths of lines and liberty of substitution, is much more appropriate. Any so-called "free verse poem" in English can be scanned, and it will be evident that, more often than not, it will be an iambic, or iambic-anapestic, poem. In those cases where it is not, the poem will be seen to fit into some other system of accentual verse, such as the *variable foot*, or *dipodics*, *Skeltonics*, or perhaps *sprung rhythm* or *Anglo-Saxon prosody*.

Many poets have said that there is no such thing as "free verse." That is true, especially in English, but we have the term, and for the time being, at least, we must use it.

Free verse, then, is a LINE of verse that does not fit into one of the three *metrical* prosodic systems, yet is distinguished from prose by its more emphatic rhythms. Free verse may also utilize alliteration, consonance, various kinds of rhymes, and other devices of versification. Note that free verse is *not* blank verse: the latter is measured, the former is not measured. Lines may be of any length, and they usually vary within a poem. The line length is often determined by the *breath pause:* logical and/or vocal phraseology.

The PROSE POEM is a poem written in prose rhythms, but whose language and imagery are heightened or intensified. POLYPHONIC PROSE may utilize other devices as well, such as assonance, internal rhyme, alliteration, etcetera, but its rhythms remain those of prose, and the poem is written in paragraphs, not lines.

The VERSE PARAGRAPH is to be distinguished from the paragraphs of a prose poem. It is a unit of lines in a metrical poem that is analogous to a paragraph of prose in that it deals with matters that have logical relationships with one another and a common focus.

NASHERS are *lines* or *couplets*, usually long, of flat free verse or prose with humorous, often multisyllabic endings utilizing wrenched rhymes. Nashers are often used satirically. For another satiric form built on an opposite metric, see SKEL-TONICS in the section concerned with SATIRICS.

The systems of Hebrew prosody have been part of our tradition at least since the King James version of the Bible was introduced. A good portion of the Bible is written in verse that, since its structure does not depend upon any kind of metric, would therefore be considered *free verse* in our system, but might better be called *grammatics*.

Hebrew prosody is structured on *parallelism*. Briefly, there are four major parallelisms:

I. SYNONYMOUS PARALLELISM—Each *verse* is broken into two halves. The first half is a complete thought; the second half *repeats* the first thought using *different words*.

II. SYNTHETIC PARALLELISM—Each *verse* is broken into two halves. The first half is a complete thought; the second half gives a *consequence* of the first thought.

III. ANTITHETICAL PARALLELISM—Each *verse* is broken into two halves. The first half is a complete thought; the second half *rebuts* the first thought.

IV. CLIMACTIC PARALLELISM—Each *verse* builds upon the preceding verse until a *climax* is attained in the last verse.

Although all poetic devices may appear in parallel construction, they are not an integral part of the system, and rhyme especially will be random, if not simply accidental.

WORD-COUNT PROSODY is a free-verse system in which each line of the first stanza is assigned a certain number of words. Succeeding stanzas retain the same word-counts as the first stanza, line for line. The system is capable of great flexibility, for syllabic lengths and number of stresses in each line may vary greatly, even in lines containing the same number of words.

GLOSE

Spanish and Portuguese. Accentual-syllabic. May be written in any meter and in any line-length. The glose *begins* with a QUATRAIN called the *texte*. There are four ensuing stanzas of ten lines each: the poem is thus forty-four lines long. Each line of the texte becomes a *refrain:* in order, line one finishes stanza one; line two finishes stanza two; line three finishes stanza three, and line four finishes stanza four, completing the poem.

The only rhyme requirement is that the *sixth* and *ninth* lines of each stanza rhyme with the refrains for that stanza; the rest of the rhyme pattern is set by the poet.

The diagram for a poem with a texte rhyming *ABAB*:

lines:	rhymes and refrains:
1.	A^1 ⎫
2.	B^1 ⎪
3.	A^2 ⎬ —*texte*
4.	B^2 ⎭
5.	
6.	
7.	
8.	
9.	
10.	a
11.	
12.	
13.	a
14.	A^1—*refrain*
15.	
16.	
17.	
18.	
19.	
20.	b

71

21.
22.
23.   b
24.   B¹—*refrain*

25.
26.
27.
28.
29.
30.   a
31.
32.
33.   a
34.   A²—*refrain*

35.
36.
37.
38.
39.
40.   b
41.
42.
43.   b
44.   B²—*refrain*

For similar forms see the RONDEAU REDOUBLÉ, the SONNET REDOUBLÉ, and the CAROL.

GWAWDODYNS

Gwawdodyn, a syllabic Welsh form, is a QUATRAIN *stanza* that has lines of nine, nine, ten, and nine syllables respectively. The *first*, *second*, and *fourth* lines end-rhyme with one another. The *third* line may rhyme internally with itself *or* there may be a syllable *before the end of the line* that rhymes *into* line *four*.

Here are two possible stanza schemes. The first method would be diagrammed thus:

lines: *syllables and rhymes:*

1.   x   x   x   x   x   x   x   x   a
2.   x   x   x   x   x   x   x   x   a
3.   x   x   x   x   *b*   x   x   x   x   b
4.   x   x   x   x   x   x   x   x   a

5.   etcetera.

The second method, which is looser, might be plotted this way:

1.   x   x   x   x   x   x   x   x   a
2.   x   x   x   x   x   x   x   x   a
3.   x   x   x   x   x   x   *b*   *x*   *x*   x
4.   *x*   *x*   *x*   *b*   x   x   x   x   a

Gwawdodyn HIR is similar except that a rhyming quatrain, each line of which contains nine syllables, is substituted for the opening couplet. Thus, instead of two lines rhyming *aa*, there would be four lines rhyming *aaaa* beginning the stanza, which would then be a SESTET.

HENDECASYLLABICS

Greek. Accentual-syllabic. A pentameter LINE of eleven syllables. Strictly, it is made up, in this order, of a trochee *or* spondee, a dactyl, and three trochees *or* two trochees and a spondee:

line:	meters:				
1.	x́x	x́xx	x́x	x́x	x́x

or:

2.	x́x́	x́xx	x́x	x́x	x́x́

HEROICS

English or Greek. Accentual-syllabic. The ENGLISH HEROIC LINE is iambic pentameter (see BLANK VERSE). A COUPLET *stanza* in this meter rhymed *aa* is called a HEROIC COUPLET. If the stanza is a QUATRAIN in this meter, it is called the HEROIC STANZA, set forms of which are the ITALIAN and the SICILIAN QUATRAIN.

The CLASSICAL HEROIC LINE is the hexameter (see ELE-GIACS).

Verses composed in either of these meters are called HEROIC VERSE.

The pattern for the heroic couplet:

lines:	meters and rhymes:				
1.	xx́	xx́	xx́	xx́	xá
2.	xx́	xx́	xx́	xx́	xá

Traditionally, the greatest heroic form is the EPIC, which is a narrative poem of great length dealing with matters of large import and grand proportion.

For other heroic forms see HEROIC OCTAVE and HEROIC RISPETTO in the section dealing with the RISPETTO, the heroic SESTET and SONNET, and CHANSON DE GESTE.

HIR A THODDAID

Welsh. Syllabic. A SESTET *stanza*. Line five has a count of ten syllables. The other five lines each contain nine syllables. Lines one, two, three, four, and six rhyme. A syllable toward the end of line five cross-rhymes *into* the middle of line six. Scheme:

lines:	*syllables and rhymes:*
1.	x x x x x x x x a
2.	x x x x x x x x a
3.	x x x x x x x x a
4.	x x x x x x x x a
5.	x x x x x x *x* *b* *x* *x*
6.	x x x *b* *x* *x* x x a
7.	etcetera.

KYRIELLE

French. Syllabic. A poem written in QUATRAIN *stanzas*. Each line has a count of eight syllables. The last line of the first quatrain is the *refrain*, and it reappears as the last line of each quatrain. Usually it is rhymed. The poem may have any number of stanzas.

A possible plot:

lines:	*syllables and rhymes:*
1.	x x x x x x x a
2.	x x x x x x x b
3.	x x x x x x x a
4.	x x x x x x x B—*refrain*
5.	x x x x x x x x c
6.	x x x x x x x x b
7.	x x x x x x x x c
8.	x x x x x x x B—*refrain*
9.	etcetera.

LAI

A French form or stanza pattern. Syllabic. A poem *or* stanza of nine lines turning on two rhymes: *aabaabaab*. The *a* lines are five syllables long; the *b* lines are two syllables long.

In a poem consisting of more than one stanza, following stanzas have their own rhymes.

A diagram for one stanza:

lines:	syllables and rhymes:
1.	x x x x a
2.	x x x x a
3.	x b
4.	x x x x a
5.	x x x x a
6.	x b
7.	x x x x a
8.	x x x x a
9.	x b

The LAI NOUVEAU, also French and syllabic, is a development of the *lai*. More complicated than the *lai*, the opening *a* lines of the *lai nouveau* form a refrain for later stanzas alternately as in the VILLANELLE. The A¹ line closes stanza II; A² closes stanza III, and so on to the last stanza, where they are united in a couplet, *in reverse order*, to close the poem: A²A¹. Though the *main* rhyme is usually carried from stanza to stanza, sometimes the short-line rhymes vary from stanza to stanza.

The schematic for a strict poem consisting of four eight-line stanzas would be plotted thus:

lines:	syllables, rhymes, refrains:
1.	x x x x A¹—*refrain*
2.	x x x x A²—*refrain*
3.	x b
4.	x x x x a
5.	x x x x a

6.	x	b			
7.	x	x	x	x	a
8.	x	x	x	x	a
9.	x	x	x	x	a
10.	x	x	x	x	a
11.	x	b			
12.	x	x	x	x	a
13.	x	x	x	x	a
14.	x	b			
15.	x	x	x	x	a
16.	x	x	x	x	A¹—*refrain*
17.	x	x	x	x	a
18.	x	x	x	x	a
19.	x	b			
20.	x	x	x	x	a
21.	x	x	x	x	a
22.	x	b			
23.	x	x	x	x	a
24.	x	x	x	x	A²—*refrain*
25.	x	x	x	x	a
26.	x	x	x	x	a
27.	x	b			
28.	x	x	x	x	a
29.	x	x	x	x	a
30.	x	b			
31.	x	x	x	x	A²—*refrain*
32.	x	x	x	x	A¹—*refrain*

The VIRELAI, like its sister forms, is a syllabic French stanza pattern. Its syllabic count is the same as the *lai*, and it has, as a rule, nine lines to the stanza, as does the *lai*. The difference is that the *long* lines of a following stanza pick up the short-line rhymes of the preceding stanza. This may be carried on indefinitely until the final stanza picks up as its short-line rhyme the long-line rhyme of the *first* stanza.

This is the pattern for a *virelai* of three stanzas:

lines:	syllables and rhymes:
1.	x x x x a
2.	x x x x a
3.	x b
4.	x x x x a
5.	x x x x a
6.	x b
7.	x x x x a
8.	x x x x a
9.	x b
10.	x x x x b
11.	x x x x b
12.	x c
13.	x x x x b
14.	x x x x b
15.	x c
16.	x x x x b
17.	x x x x b
18.	x c
19.	x x x x c
20.	x x x x c
21.	x a
22.	x x x x c
23.	x x x x c
24.	x a
25.	x x x x c
26.	x x x x c
27.	x a

For other forms that utilize this kind of interlocking rhyme see the interlocking RUBAIYAT, TERZA RIMA, and the TERZANELLE.

The LAI forms are strict, and should be distinguished from the LAY, which is not. See the section on LYRICS.

LIMERICK

French. Originally syllabic but, in English, accentual-syllabic. A single QUINTET rhyming *aabba* and written in anapestic measures. Lines one, two, and five are of three anapestic feet; lines three and four contain two anapestic feet. Line five *may* be merely a modified repetition of line one.

lines:	meters and rhymes:		
1.	xxx́	xxx́	xxá
2.	xxx́	xxx́	xxá
3.	xxx́	xxb́	
4.	xxx́	xxb́	
5.	xxx́	xxx́	xxá

A related *stanza* form is the English MADSONG STANZA. Its rhyme scheme is $a^3b^3c^2c^2b^3$, its meters, susceptible to considerable variation, are usually iambic, trochaic, or dipodic, and the long lines often end either in spondees or with an extra unaccented syllable (i.e., the long lines often utilize feminine endings). See also *dipodics* and *sprung rhythm*.

The limerick is a form used primarily as a vehicle for nonsense verse. Like the EPIGRAM, it often turns on wit or word-play. The madsong is traditionally utilized as its name indicates—it is a *lyric* sung by a fool or madman.

LYRICS

A number of loose verse forms exist that have traditionally been used in certain lyric, or songlike contexts:

The ALBA or AUBADE is a love lyric that has *dawn* as its setting or subject.

ANACREONTICS are songs in praise of wine, women, and song. The meter is often trochaic tetrameter.

The CANSO or CANZO or CANZONE is a song about love and/or beauty.

A CANTICLE is a song derived from liturgy.

The CAROL is a joyous hymn; there is also a set form.

The CHANT is a work song or religious recitative that utilizes a *refrain*. See the CHANT ROYAL for a set form.

A CHANTEY is a sailor's work song.

The DITHYRAMB is a frenzied and raucous hymn in honor of revelry.

The ELEGY is a reflection upon *death* or some other equally serious subject. The DIRGE, THRENODY, or MONODY are similar, but are usually more intense songs of lamentation.

The EPITHALAMION is a lyric written in honor of a *wedding*. A *meditative* lyric upon the same subject is a PROTHALAMION.

The LAY is a short narrative song that is usually written in four-beat couplets. It is *not* to be confused with the French LAI, which is a set form.

The MADRIGAL is a lyric, usually about love, to be set to music. There is also a set form.

MADSONG (see the LIMERICK).

A NURSERY RHYME is any song, jingle, nonsense verse, or doggerel that is traditionally used for the entertainment of children. See also *dipodics* and *sprung rhythm*.

The ODE is a lyric, often occasional, written on a level, and in a tone of exaltation. There are set forms.

PALINODE (listed separately).

The PASTORAL or IDYL is a poem ostensibly about or set in the countryside, usually with shepherds or other rural types of people as the prime figures. However, it is often concerned with matters of more general or graver import.

The ECLOGUE is a pastoral cast in the form of a dialogue (see DRAMATICS). The PASTORAL ELEGY is a combination of the two lyric forms.

RIDDLE (see DIDACTICS).

The ROMANCE (or METRICAL ROMANCE, to distinguish it from prose) is a verse tale whose subject matter concerns *chivalry* or *honor*.

A ROUNDELAY is any simple lyric that utilizes a refrain. See RONDELET.

The RUNE is a poem of *incantation* or magic. It is often an ACROSTIC or an anagram.

The SERENADE is similar to the ALBA except that its setting is the *evening*.

The SIRVENTE is a lyric *satire* on either public matters or religion.

MADRIGAL

Italian and English. Accentual-syllabic. Written in lines of either seven or eleven syllables, the madrigal is comprised of two *or* three triplets, followed by one *or* two rhyming couplets. There is no set rhyme scheme for the triplets, but if the poem were written in TERZA RIMA it might look like this:

lines:	rhymes:
1.	a
2.	b
3.	a
4.	b
5.	c
6.	b
7.	c
8.	d
9.	c
10.	d
11.	d
12.	a
13.	a

For freer forms, see the section concerning LYRICS.

MOTE

Spanish. A mote is any poem complete in one or two lines, containing a complete statement or thought. The mote may serve as a *texte* to be glossed in verse (as a quatrain is glossed in the GLOSE).

There are any number of set single-line forms that might serve as motes, including the ALEXANDRINE, SEPTENARY, and the CLASSICAL HEROIC LINE.

See also the COUPLET.

OCTAVE

A *stanza* consisting of eight lines. It may be written in any meter, rhymed or unrhymed. Lines may be of any length. Rhymes, if any, may be random or regular.

The ITALIAN OCTAVE is written in iambic pentameter lines, and it rhymes *abbaabba* (see the Italian SONNET).

The SICILIAN OCTAVE is accentual-syllabic also. It is a *stanza* of iambic pentameter lines turning on two rhymes. It may also be a complete poem.

The diagram for the Sicilian octave:

lines:	*meters and rhymes:*
1.	xx́ xx́ xx́ xx́ xá
2.	xx́ xx́ xx́ xx́ xb́
3.	xx́ xx́ xx́ xx́ xá
4.	xx́ xx́ xx́ xx́ xb́
5.	xx́ xx́ xx́ xx́ xá
6.	xx́ xx́ xx́ xx́ xb́
7.	xx́ xx́ xx́ xx́ xá
8.	xx́ xx́ xx́ xx́ xb́

The STRAMBOTTO is a Sicilian octave in hendecasyllabic lines.

For closely related forms see the Italian OCTAVE above, OTTAVA RIMA, the Sicilian SESTET, and the second ending of the Italian SONNET. See also the remarks concerning the HEROIC OCTAVE in the section dealing with the RISPETTO.

ODE

There are three more or less strict forms of the ode. The first is the PINDARIC ODE, which is of Greek origin. It is usually written in accentual-syllabic verse. The stanza pattern, rhyme scheme, and line lengths are determined by the poet.

The poem is divided into three *movements*, not necessarily stanzas. The *first movement*, called the *strophe*, and the *second movement*, called the *antistrophe*, are identical and strict in form, though the exact form is devised by the poet.

The *third* and last movement of the poem is called the *stand* or *epode*. Its form is strict also, but entirely different from that of the first two movements.

The ENGLISH ODE (or Keatsian ode) is accentual-syllabic. It consists of three ten-line iambic pentameter stanzas. Stanza one rhymes *ababcdecde:* stanzas two and three have the same scheme but their own rhymes.

The pattern for one stanza of the English ode:

lines:	*meters and rhymes:*				
1.	xx́	xx́	xx́	xx́	xá
2.	xx́	xx́	xx́	xx́	xb́
3.	xx́	xx́	xx́	xx́	xá
4.	xx́	xx́	xx́	xx́	xb́
5.	xx́	xx́	xx́	xx́	xć
6.	xx́	xx́	xx́	xx́	xd́
7.	xx́	xx́	xx́	xx́	xé
8.	xx́	xx́	xx́	xx́	xć
9.	xx́	xx́	xx́	xx́	xd́
10.	xx́	xx́	xx́	xx́	xé

The stanza pattern for the English ode was derived by combining elements of the English and Italian SONNET forms: a Sicilian QUATRAIN from the English sonnet (*abab*) is attached to an Italian SESTET (*cdecde*).

The HOMOSTROPHIC ODE (or Horatian ode) consists of any number of *formal* stanzas. However, the form of the stanzas is determined by the poet.

A fourth type, the Cowleyan or IRREGULAR ODE is a loose form, and it may be described simply as a serious LYRIC. Its structure, too, is determined by the poet.

A RONSARDIAN ODE is, strictly speaking, a *stanza form*. Such an ode may be of any length, provided each stanza is nine lines long, rhymes *ababccddc*, and varies its line-lengths between pentameter and dimeter iambic lines, in a specific order. The *last* line is a *tetrameter* line:

lines:	*meters and rhymes:*				
1.	xx́	xx́	xx́	xx́	xá
2.	xx́	xb́			
3.	xx́	xx́	xx́	xx́	xá
4.	xx́	xb́			
5.	xx́	xx́	xx́	xx́	xć
6.	xx́	xx́	xx́	xx́	xć
7.	xx́	xd̂			
8.	xx́	xd̂			
9.	xx́	xx́	xx́	xć	

OTTAVA RIMA

An Italian *stanza* pattern. It may also be a complete poem. It is an OCTAVE stanza in iambic pentameter lines rhyming *abababcc*.

The scheme:

lines:	meters and rhymes:
1.	xx́ xx́ xx́ xx́ xá
2.	xx́ xx́ xx́ xx́ xb́
3.	xx́ xx́ xx́ xx́ xá
4.	xx́ xx́ xx́ xx́ xb́
5.	xx́ xx́ xx́ xx́ xá
6.	xx́ xx́ xx́ xx́ xb́
7.	xx́ xx́ xx́ xx́ xć
8.	xx́ xx́ xx́ xx́ xć

Essentially, *ottava rima* is a Sicilian SESTET expanded by the addition of a HEROIC COUPLET.

For related forms see the Italian OCTAVE and the Sicilian OCTAVE. See also the remarks concerning the HEROIC OCTAVE in the section on the RISPETTO.

PALINODE

A Greek and Italian form. A palinode is a lyric, a "song of retraction" for a derogatory statement that has been made. A set form consists of *two strophes* and *two antistrophes*. These are of no traditional pattern but, as in the ODE, the poet sets a pattern that must be adhered to throughout the poem.

The pattern of the first strophe is mirrored in the last antistrophe; the pattern of the second strophe is mirrored in the first antistrophe, thus: strophe *A*, strophe *B*, antistrophe *B*, antistrophe *A*, in that order. The two strophes may be the statement, and the two antistrophes may be the retraction.

Technically, the two (differing) strophes are called the *ode*, and the two (differing) antistrophes are the "palinode" proper.

PANTOUM

A Malayan form. Accentual-syllabic. Lines may be of any length in any meter. A *pantoum* consists of an indefinite number of QUATRAIN stanzas with particular restrictions: lines two and four of each stanza, *in their entirety*, become lines one and three of the following stanza, and so on. These carry-over lines are called *repetons*. The rhyme scheme is *abab*, *bcbc*, etcetera.

The poem may be ended in one of two ways: either in a QUATRAIN whose repetons are lines one and three of the *first* stanza *in reversed order*; or the poem may end in a repeton couplet consisting of lines one and three of the first stanza *in reversed order*.

The pattern for a four-stanza poem:

lines:	*rhymes and repetons:*	
1.	A^1	
2.	B^1	
3.	A^2	
4.	B^2	
5.	B^1	
6.	C^1	
7.	B^2	
8.	C^2	
9.	C^1	
10.	D^1	
11.	C^2	
12.	D^2	
13.	Z^1 *or* A^2	
14.	A^2	A^1
15.	Z^2	
16.	A^1	

For another form that uses repetons, see the TERZANELLE.

PEARLINE STANZA

English. Accentual or accentual-syllabic. A twelve-line stanza written either with four *accents* to the line or in tetrameters. Alliteration, if written in accentual verse, as in ANGLO-SAXON PROSODY. The stanza turns on three rhymes and line *twelve* is a variable *refrain* that is carried through *two or more* stanzas. The *last word or phrase*, however, is constant for as long as the refrain is carried. The rhyme scheme is *ababababbcbC*.

A possible pattern for one stanza in accentuals:

lines:	words, syllables, alliterations, accents, caesuras, rhymes, refrains:
1.	ó óx · x óx xá
2.	x ṕx ṕx · x ṕ x b́
3.	q́ x q́xx · x q́x á
4.	x ŕx x ŕx · x ŕx b́
5.	x ś x śx · x ś xá
6.	x t́ x t́ · x t́x b́
7.	xú xxxú · x x ú á
8.	x v́ x v́xx · x v́ x b́
9.	xẃ x ẃ · x ẃ x b́
10.	x f́ x f́ · x f́ x ć
11.	x ýx x ýx · x ýxb́
12.	x x źx ź · xźx C̆—*refrain*
13.	etcetera.

For further information concerning the Pearline stanza, see *sprung rhythm*.

POULTER'S MEASURE

English. Accentual-syllabic. Rhymed. A COUPLET that alternates the ALEXANDRINE (see also SPENSERIAN STANZA) and the *septenary* or FOURTEENER. There may be any number of couplets in a stanza or poem.

The Alexandrine is a LINE of iambic hexameter verse:

$$x\acute{x} \quad x\acute{x} \quad x\acute{x} \quad x\acute{x} \quad x\acute{x} \quad x\acute{x}.$$

The fourteener was, in Latin verse, a LINE consisting of seven metrical feet. In English verse the line contains fourteen syllables arranged in iambics, with a caesura appearing somewhere in the center of the line:

$$x\acute{x} \quad x\acute{x} \quad x\acute{x} \quad x\acute{x} \quad \cdot \quad x\acute{x} \quad x\acute{x} \quad x\acute{x}$$

A schematic of one couplet of Poulter's measure:

lines: *meters, caesuras, and rhymes:*

1. $x\acute{x} \quad x\acute{x} \quad x\acute{x} \quad x\acute{x} \quad x\acute{x} \quad x\acute{a}$
2. $x\acute{x} \quad x\acute{x} \quad x\acute{x} \quad x\acute{x} \quad \cdot \quad x\acute{x} \quad x\acute{x} \quad x\acute{a}$

QUATRAIN

A stanza or poem consisting of four lines. It may be written in any meter and line-length, and it may be rhymed or unrhymed.

The ENVELOPE STANZA is a quatrain stanza that rhymes *abba*. The so-called IN MEMORIAM STANZA is an iambic tetrameter envelope.

The REDONDILLA, a Spanish form of the envelope stanza, is an *octosyllabic* quatrain rhyming *abba*.

The ITALIAN QUATRAIN is an envelope stanza that is written in iambic pentameter measures:

lines:	meters and rhymes:
1.	xx́ xx́ xx́ xx́ xá
2.	xx́ xx́ xx́ xx́ xb́
3.	xx́ xx́ xx́ xx́ xb́
4.	xx́ xx́ xx́ xx́ xá

Doubled, it becomes the ITALIAN OCTAVE, which is utilized in the Italian SONNET. The Italian quatrain is a form of HEROIC STANZA.

The SICILIAN QUATRAIN is also a set form of the HEROIC STANZA, and is the pattern for the quatrains found in the ENGLISH SONNET. It is the same as the Italian octave, except that it rhymes *abab*. Doubled, it becomes the Sicilian OCTAVE.

For other set forms and uses of the quatrain see the sections on AE FREISLIGHE, ALCAICS, AWDL GYWYDD, BALLAD STANZA, BYR A THODDAID, CASBAIRDNE, COMMON MEASURE, DEIBHIDHE, the ENGLYNS, GWAWDODYN, KYRIELLE, PANTOUM, the RANNAIGHEACHTS, RIONNAIRD TRI N-ARD, RISPETTO, ROUNDEL, RUBAI, SAPPHICS, SÉADNA, SNEADHBHAIRDNE, and TODDAID.

QUINTET

A poem or stanza consisting of five lines. It may be in any meter and line-length, rhymed or unrhymed.

The SICILIAN QUINTET is written in iambic pentameter measures, and it rhymes *ababa*.

The pattern:

lines:	meters and rhymes:
1.	xx́ xx́ xx́ xx́ xá
2.	xx́ xx́ xx́ xx́ xb́
3.	xx́ xx́ xx́ xx́ xá
4.	xx́ xx́ xx́ xx́ xb́
5.	xx́ xx́ xx́ xx́ xá

The QUINTILLA, a Spanish form, is any *octosyllabic* quintet rhyming *ababa*, *abbab*, *abaab*, *aabab*, or *aabba*.

For other set forms of the quintet see the sections on the CINQUAIN, LIMERICK, and TANKA.

RANNAIGHEACHTS

Irish. Syllabic.

RANNAIGHEACHT GHAIRID is a QUATRAIN *stanza*. The first line is three syllables long, the rest are seven syllables in length. The quatrain single-rhymes *aaba*. Line *three* cross-rhymes with line *four*.

In *all* the Irish forms in this section and elsewhere, the *poem* (not the stanza) ends with the same first syllable, word, or line with which it begins.

The diagram for one stanza:

lines:	*syllables and rhymes:*
1.	x x a
2.	x x x x x x a
3.	x x x x x x b
4.	x *x* *b* *x* *x* x a
5.	etcetera.

When the lines in this form end in *disyllables* instead of monosyllables, it is called RANDAIGECHT CHETHARCHUBAID GARIT RÉCOMARCACH.

RANNAIGHEACHT MHÓR is a QUATRAIN *stanza* of seven-syllable lines *consonating*, not rhyming, *abab*. There are at least two cross-rhymes in each couplet, and the final word of line *three* rhymes with a word in the interior of line *four*. The internal rhyme in the first couplet may be slant-rhyme. In the *second* couplet the rhymes *must* be exact. Two words alliterate in each line, the final word of line *four* alliterating with the preceding stressed word.

A simplified schematic:

lines:	*syllables, cross-rhymes, and consonates:*	
1.	x x x x b x ac	*—lines 1 and 3,*
2.	x x x a x x bc	*2 and 4* CONSO-
3.	x b x x x x ac	NATE, *not rhyme*
4.	x x a x x x bc	

RANNAIGHEACHT BHEAG is the same, except the line endings are disyllabic.

DEACHNADH MÓR is also the same, except that lines *one* and *three* are octosyllabic, lines *two* and *four* are hexasyllabic, and all line endings are disyllabic words.

Welsh. Syllabic. A LINE of three, four, *or* five sections.
Each section contains four syllables. All but the last section
rhyme with each other. The last section carries the *main*
rhyme from line to line (or from stanza to stanza, depending
on how the lines are set up: i.e., each section may be written
on the page as a single line of verse).

In this pattern, each section is treated as one line, and
each set of sections is treated as one stanza:

lines (or sections):   *syllables and rhymes:*

1.	x	x	x	a
2.	x	x	x	a
3.	x	x	x	a
4.	x	x	x	B

—*one line*

5.	x	x	x	c
6.	x	x	x	c
7.	x	x	x	c
8.	x	x	x	B

—*one line*

    9.   etcetera.

After two lines (sets of sections) the main rhyme may
change.

TAWDDGYRCH CADWYNOG is similarly a LINE of three,
four, *or* five sections. Each section contains four syllables.
The rhyme scheme is *abbc*. Each section must rhyme with
its *corresponding* section in at least one other line of verse. If
desired, each section may be written as one *line* of verse.

In the following schematic diagram each section is treated
as one line, and each set of sections is treated as one stanza:

lines (or sections):   *syllables and rhymes:*

1.	x	x	x	a
2.	x	x	x	b
3.	x	x	x	b
4.	x	x	x	c

—*one line*

```
5.                x  x  x  a ⎫
6.                x  x  x  b ⎬
7.                x  x  x  b ⎬ —one line
8.                x  x  x  c ⎭

9.                etcetera.
```

After two lines (or sets of sections) the rhymes may change.

RIME COUÉE

French. Syllabic. A sestet *stanza* made of two couplets of any length and two shorter lines. One of the short lines follows each couplet. The short lines rhyme with each other.

A schematic diagram of *rime couée* in iambics:

lines:	*meters and rhymes*:			
1.	xx́	xx́	xx́	xá
2.	xx́	xx́	xx́	xá
3.	xx́	xx́	xb́	
4.	xx́	xx́	xx́	xć
5.	xx́	xx́	xx́	xć
6.	xx́	xx́	xb́	
7.	etcetera.			

The Scottish Burns stanza, or standard habbie, a variation, rhymes $a^4a^4a^4b^2a^4b^2$.

For similar forms see the sections on the lai and common particular measure.

RIME ROYAL

A Scottish form. Accentual-syllabic. A septet *stanza* rhyming *ababbcc*. The lines are written in iambic pentameter measures.

Diagram:

lines:	*meters and rhymes:*				
1.	xx́	xx́	xx́	xx́	xá
2.	xx́	xx́	xx́	xx́	xb́
3.	xx́	xx́	xx́	xx́	xá
4.	xx́	xx́	xx́	xx́	xb́
5.	xx́	xx́	xx́	xx́	xb́
6.	xx́	xx́	xx́	xx́	xć
7.	xx́	xx́	xx́	xx́	xć
8.	etcetera.				

RIONNAIRD TRI N-ARD

Irish. Syllabic. A QUATRAIN *stanza* of hexasyllabic lines with disyllabic endings. Lines *two* and *four* rhyme, and line *three* consonates with them. There are two cross-rhymes in the second couplet, none in the first. There is alliteration in each line, and the last syllable of line *one* alliterates with the first accented word of line *two*. There are two cross-rhymes in the second couplet, none in the first.

The *poem* (not the stanza) ends with the same first syllable, word, or line with which it begins.

lines:	*syllables and rhymes:*
1.	x x x x <u>x a</u>
2.	x x x x <u>x bc</u>
3.	x b x x <u>x c</u>
4.	x x c x <u>x bc</u>
5.	etcetera.

—line 3 CONSONATES *with 2 and 4*

RISPETTO

An Italian form. Accentual-syllabic. Any complete poem consisting of two rhyming QUATRAINS. Strict versions combine a Sicilian QUATRAIN and an Italian QUATRAIN. Another version has the *rispetto* rhyming *abab ccdd*. Many *rispettos* are written in iambic tetrameter measures:

lines:	meters and rhymes:			
1.	xx́	xx́	xx́	xá
2.	xx́	xx́	xx́	xb́
3.	xx́	xx́	xx́	xá
4.	xx́	xx́	xx́	xb́
5.	xx́	xx́	xx́	xć
6.	xx́	xx́	xx́	xć
7.	xx́	xx́	xx́	xd́
8.	xx́	xx́	xx́	xd́

If the *rispetto* is written in iambic pentameter, it will be seen that it can combine heroic forms—the Sicilian and Italian quatrains, or a Sicilian quatrain and two heroic couplets. It is thus a HEROIC RISPETTO.

The RISPETTO STANZA rhmes *abababcc*. If it is written in iambic pentameter it is a HEROIC OCTAVE.

A SONETTO RISPETTO combines one heroic octave with either an Italian or Sicilian SESTET.

RONDEAU

French. Syllabic. Lines may be of any length. Fifteen lines divided into three stanzas: one QUINTET, one QUATRAIN, and one SESTET. The poem turns on two rhymes and is built on one *refrain*. The refrain consists of *the first few words of the first line*.

In this pattern the refrain is represented by the letter *R*:

lines:	rhymes and refrains:
1.	. . . R a—*first line* CONTAINS *refrain*
2.	a
3.	b
4.	b
5.	a
6.	a
7.	a
8.	b
9.	. . . R
10.	a
11.	a
12.	b
13.	b
14.	a
15.	. . . R

The RONDEAU PRIME consists of twelve lines divided into two stanzas that rhyme *RabbaabR abbaR*. The *refrain* is the *first word of the first line;* it reappears as line seven and again as line twelve, ending the poem.

The pattern of the *rondeau prime:*

lines:	rhymes and refrains:
1.	. . . R a—*refrain is the first word*
2.	b
3.	b
4.	a
5.	a

| 6. | b |
| 7. | . . . R   —*refrain* |

8.	a
9.	b
10.	b
11.	a
12.	. . . R —*refrain*

The RONDEAU REDOUBLÉ consists of twenty-five lines divided into five QUATRAINS and one QUINTET. Stanza one rhymes $RA^1B^1A^2B^2$; each line in this first quatrain, which is called the *texte*, is a refrain. A *fifth refrain* consists of the *first phrase of the first line*. Thus, in all, the texte contains five refrains.

The first phrase of line one (represented by the letter R) reappears as the unrhymed line twenty-five, which ends the poem; the entire first line of the poem (A^1) reappears as line eight, ending the second stanza; line two (B^1) reappears as line twelve, ending the third stanza; line three (A^2) reappears as line sixteen, ending the fourth stanza; line four (B^2) reappears as line twenty, ending the fifth stanza.

The diagram:

	lines:	*rhymes and refrains:*
	1.	. . . R A¹—1*st line* CONTAINS *a refrain and* IS *one*
Texte—	2.	B¹—*refrain*
	3.	A²—*refrain*
	4.	B²—*refrain*
	5.	b
	6.	a
	7.	b
	8.	A¹—*refrain*
	9.	a
	10.	b
	11.	a
	12.	B¹—*refrain*

13.	b
14.	a
15.	b
16.	A²—*refrain*
17.	a
18.	b
19.	a
20.	B²—*refrain*
21.	b
22.	a
23.	b
24.	a
25.	. . . R

For a similar form, see the GLOSE, also the SONNET REDOUBLÉ and the CAROL.

RONDEL

French. Syllabic. Thirteen lines of any length divided into three stanzas: two QUATRAINS and one QUINTET. The poem turns on two rhymes and is built on a two-line refrain. The first line reappears as line seven, and as line thirteen, which ends the poem. The second line reappears as line eight, which ends the second stanza.

The schematic diagram:

lines:	rhymes and refrains:
1.	A—*refrain*
2.	B—*refrain*
3.	b
4.	a
5.	a
6.	b
7.	A
8.	B
9.	a
10.	b
11.	b
12.	a
13.	A—*refrain*

The RONDEL PRIME is one line longer. The double refrain forms lines thirteen and fourteen; thus, the last stanza would be a SESTET instead of a quintet, and the scheme would look like this:

9.	a
10.	b
11.	b
12.	a
13.	A—*refrain*
14.	B—*refrain*

RONDELET

French. Syllabic. A SEPTET *poem*. The *first* line is a refrain, which reappears as lines three and seven. The refrain is four syllables in length. The rest of the lines (two, four, five, and six) are eight syllables in length. Line four rhymes with the refrain. Lines two, five, and six have their own rhyme. Scheme:

lines:	syllables, rhymes, and refrains:
1.	x x x A
2.	x x x x x x x b
3.	x x x A
4.	x x x x x x x a
5.	x x x x x x x b
6.	x x x x x x x b
7.	x x x A

See ROUNDELAY among the LYRICS.

ROUNDEL

An English form. Accentual-syllabic. Lines may be of any length. Eleven lines broken into three stanzas: a QUATRAIN, a TRIPLET, and a QUATRAIN, in that order. The poem turns on two rhymes and is built on one *refrain*. The refrain consists of the *first word or group of words* in the first line. The refrain (R) *rhymes internally* with the *last word of the second line*. Short scheme: $R^b abaR^b$ *bab abaR^b*.

The diagram:

lines:	rhymes and refrain:	
1.	R^b	a—*1st line contains rhyming refrain*
2.		b
3.		a
4.	R^b	—*refrain*
5.		b
6.		a
7.		b
8.		a
9.		b
10.		a
11.	R^b	—*refrain*

Arabic. Accentual-syllabic. A complete poem consisting of one QUATRAIN rhyming *aaba*. Lines are often tetrameter or pentameter, and all are of the same length:

lines:	meters and rhymes:			
1.	xx́	xx́	xx́	xá
2.	xx́	xx́	xx́	xá
3.	xx́	xx́	xx́	xb́
4.	xx́	xx́	xx́	xá

A RUBAIYAT is a poem composed of a number of these quatrains utilized as stanzas.

In the INTERLOCKING RUBAIYAT the end-sound of line *three* in the first stanza becomes the rhyme in the second stanza; the same is true for succeeding stanzas, each of which picks up its rhyme from the third line of the preceding stanza. In the *last* stanza the third line takes its end-sound from the rhyme of the first stanza.

The diagram for a four-stanza poem:

lines:	rhymes:
1.	a
2.	a
3.	b
4.	a
5.	b
6.	b
7.	c
8.	b
9.	c
10.	c
11.	d
12.	c

13.   d
14.   d
15.   a
16.   d

For other forms that use interlocking rhyme see TERZA RIMA and the TERZANELLE.

SAPPHICS

A Greek form. Accentual-syllabic. Unrhymed. In English meters, a SAPPHIC LINE consists of eleven syllables and five verse feet, the central foot being a dactyl; the other four feet, two on either side of the central dactyl, are trochees.

A SAPPHIC STANZA is composed of three such lines plus one that is shorter, called an ADONIC: one dactyl followed by one trochee.

The rhythms of each line are *falling rhythms*: the accents of all verse feet fall on the *first* syllable—the endings of the lines are consequently *feminine endings*. The opposite of this, in which the accents fall on the last syllable of all verse feet, is called *rising rhythm*, and the line endings would be *masculine*.

There may be any number of stanzas in a Sapphic poem: the stanzas are QUATRAINS.

A spondee *may* be substituted for a trochee in lines one and two, feet two and five; and in line three, foot five—see the *italicized* sections of the diagram:

lines:	meters:				
1.	x́x	*x́x*	x́xx	x́x	*x́x*
2.	x́x	*x́x*	x́xx	x́x	*x́x*
3.	x́x	x́x	x́xx	x́x	*x́x*
4.	x́xx	x́x			

SATIRICS

There are three forms that are often used in a satirical context.

The EPIGRAM is accentual-syllabic as a rule. It is a brief, usually rhymed poem on a single idea with an inversion or shift in thought that focuses on wit, satire, or some other intellectual gambit. It is perhaps better described as terse verse with a cutting edge. Epigrams have no set form, though they are often quatrains or couplets.

The EPITAPH is similar except that it is (ostensibly) an inscription for a tomb. The literary epitaph, like the epigram, often focuses on wit or satire and might be described as terse verse for the long gone.

SKELTONICS are short, usually dipodic or tripodic (two–foot or three-foot) *lines*, insistently and humorously rhymed, utilizing heavily accented rhythms and alliteration for satiric effect. Skeltonics are sometimes called *tumbling verse*. See also *dipodics* and *sprung rhythm*.

HUDIBRASTICS are irregular octosyllabic or tetrametric lines, humorously rhymed in couplets.

Another satiric line is the NASHER, which will be found in the section dealing with FREE VERSE.

The FABLIAU, a French form, is a short verse narrative, usually in octosyllabic couplets (see HUDIBRASTICS, above, and CYHYDEDD FER), that takes its material from the middle classes.

Such forms as Skeltonics, Hudibrastics, and Nashers are modes of DOGGEREL verse. Generally speaking, doggerel is any irregularly structured verse broad in its comic effect and aimed primarily at caricature and burlesque.

Any form may be used satirically. When this occurs, the word *mock* is usually prefixed to the name of the form, as in "mock-epic," "mock-ode," and so forth.

Irish. Syllabic. A QUATRAIN stanza of alternating octo-syllabic lines with disyllabic endings, and heptasyllabic lines with monosyllabic endings. Lines *two* and *four* rhyme; line *three* rhymes with the stressed word preceding the final word of line *four*. There are two cross-rhymes in the second couplet. There is alliteration in each line, the final word of line *four* alliterating with the preceding stressed word. The final syllable of line *one* alliterates with the first stressed word of line *two*.

The *poem* (not the stanza) ends with the same first syllable, word, or line with which it begins.

A simplified version:

lines:	*syllables and rhymes:*
1.	x x x x x x x x a
2.	x x x x x x b
3.	x x x *x* *c* *x* x c
4.	x b x c x x b

SÉADNA MÓR is the same except that lines *two* and *four* have trisyllabic endings.

SEPTET

A stanza *or* poem consisting of seven lines in any meter, rhymed or unrhymed.

The SICILIAN SEPTET is written in iambic pentameter measures rhyming *abababa:*

lines:	meters and rhymes:
1.	xx́ xx́ xx́ xx́ xá
2.	xx́ xx́ xx́ xx́ xb́
3.	xx́ xx́ xx́ xx́ xá
4.	xx́ xx́ xx́ xx́ xb́
5.	xx́ xx́ xx́ xx́ xá
6.	xx́ xx́ xx́ xx́ xb́
7.	xx́ xx́ xx́ xx́ xá

For other set forms and uses of the septet see the sections on RIME ROYAL and the RONDELET.

A stanza *or* poem consisting of six lines in any meter, rhymed or unrhymed.

The ITALIAN SESTET is written in iambic pentameter measures, and it rhymes *abcabc*.

The SICILIAN SESTET is the same, but it rhymes *ababab:*

lines:	meters and rhymes:				
1.	xx́	xx́	xx́	xx́	xá
2.	xx́	xx́	xx́	xx́	xb́
3.	xx́	xx́	xx́	xx́	xá
4.	xx́	xx́	xx́	xx́	xb́
5.	xx́	xx́	xx́	xx́	xá
6.	xx́	xx́	xx́	xx́	xb́

A HEROIC SESTET is written in iambic pentameter measures and rhymes *ababcc*.

The SEXTILLA, a Spanish form, is an *octosyllablic* sestet rhyming either *aabccb* or *ababcc*.

A sestet that utilizes the BOB (see BOB AND WHEEL) is the Scottish BURNS STANZA or STANDARD HABBIE (see RIME COUÉE).

For various uses and relatives of these forms see the SICILIAN OCTAVE, OTTAVA RIMA, ITALIAN SONNET, and SONETTO RISPETTO.

SESTINA

French. Syllabic. Thirty-nine lines divided into six SESTETS and one TRIPLET, which is called the *envoy*. The poem is ordinarily unrhymed. Instead of rhymes, the six *end-words* of the lines in stanza one are picked up and re-used *in a particular order*, as end-words in the remaining stanzas. In the envoy, which ends the poem, the six end-words are also picked up: *one* end-word is buried in each line, and *one* end-word finishes each line. Lines may be of any length.

The order in which the end-words are re-used is prescribed by a set pattern as follows:

lines:	*repeated end-words:*
1.	A
2.	B
3.	C
4.	D
5.	E
6.	F
7.	F
8.	A
9.	E
10.	B
11.	D
12.	C
13.	C
14.	F
15.	D
16.	A
17.	B
18.	E
19.	E
20.	C
21.	B

22.	F	
23.	A	
24.	D	
25.	D	
26.	E	
27.	A	
28.	C	
29.	F	
30.	B	
31.	B	
32.	D	
33.	F	
34.	E	
35.	C	
36.	A	
37.	B	E
38.	D	C ⎫ —envoy
39.	F	A ⎭

The rationale behind the sequence of recurring end-words seems to lie in the numerological sequence of numbers 615243. If this set of numbers is applied to *each* stanza's set of end-words, it will be seen that preceding end-words appear in the succeeding stanza in this order. Thus, apply the set of numbers, for instance to stanza two:

stanza 2:	*numbers:*	*equals stanza 3:*
F	6	C
A	1	F
E	5	D
B	2	A
D	4	B
C	3	E

What the numerological significance of the set is, however, has evidently been lost since the Middle Ages, though the form is still a popular one.

SNEADHBHAIRDNE

Irish. Syllabic. A QUATRAIN *stanza* of alternating octo-syllabic and quadrasyllabic lines ending in disyllabic words. Lines *two* and *four* rhyme, line *three* consonates with them. Every stressed word in line *four* must rhyme. Alliteration as in RIONNAIRD TRI N-ARD.

The *poem* (not the stanza) ends with the same first syllable, word, or line with which it begins.

lines:	*syllables and rhymes:*
1.	x x x x x x <u>x a</u>
2.	x x <u>x b</u>
3.	x x x x x x <u>x c</u>
4.	b b <u>x b</u>

115

Accentual-syllabic. Roughly speaking, any fourteen-line poem written in rhymed iambic pentameter verse. However, there are two basic traditional patterns of the sonnet.

The Petrarchan or ITALIAN SONNET is divided into an OCTAVE and a SESTET. The octave's rhyme is *abba abba* (see ITALIAN OCTAVE). The sestet's rhyme varies, but it is generally either *cde cde* (ITALIAN SESTET) or *cdcdcd* (SICILIAN SESTET):

lines:	meters and rhymes:								
1.	xx́	xx́	xx́	xx́	xá				
2.	xx́	xx́	xx́	xx́	xb́				
3.	xx́	xx́	xx́	xx́	xb́				
4.	xx́	xx́	xx́	xx́	xá				
5.	xx́	xx́	xx́	xx́	xá				
6.	xx́	xx́	xx́	xx́	xb́				
7.	xx́	xx́	xx́	xx́	·xb́				
8.	xx́	xx́	xx́	xx́	xá				
9.	xx́	xx́	xx́	xx́	xć	*or*	xx́	xx́	xx́ xx́ xć
10.	xx́	xx́	xx́	xx́	xd́		xx́	xx́	xx́ xx́ xd́
11.	xx́	xx́	xx́	xx́	xé		xx́	xx́	xx́ xx́ xć
12.	xx́	xx́	xx́	xx́	xć		xx́	xx́	xx́ xx́ xd́
13.	xx́	xx́	xx́	xx́	xd́		xx́	xx́	xx́ xx́ xć
14.	xx́	xx́	xx́	xx́	xé		xx́	xx́	xx́ xx́ xd́

The Shakespearian or ENGLISH SONNET is divided into three SICILIAN QUATRAINS and one HEROIC COUPLET. It is written in iambic pentameter measures:

lines:	rhymes:
1.	a
2.	b
3.	a
4.	b
5.	c
6.	d

7.	c
8.	d

9.	e
10.	f
11.	e
12.	f

13.	g
14.	g

The CROWN OF SONNETS is a sequence of seven Italian sonnets. The *last line* of each of the first six sonnets becomes the first line of the ensuing sonnet; the last line of the seventh sonnet is the first line of the first sonnet. Since the seven sonnets are considered to be one poem, no rhyme sounds or words may be re-used except in the formally repeated lines.

The SONNET REDOUBLÉ is a chain of fifteen sonnets. *Each* of the fourteen lines in the *first* sonnet (called the *texte*) becomes, in order, the *final line* in the following fourteen sonnets. A variation of this pattern makes each of the lines in the texte the *first line* in the following fourteen sonnets. For other forms that use a *texte*, see the CAROL, the GLOSE, and the RONDEAU REDOUBLÉ.

The SPENSERIAN SONNET is a chain of three SICILIAN QUATRAINS, the second and third of which pick up their first-line rhymes from the last-line rhymes of the first and second quatrains respectively, plus a HEROIC COUPLET: *abab bcbc cdcd ee*.

The tailed or CAUDATED SONNET adds two three-foote tsail and two heroic couplets to the Italian sonnet ands rhym *abbaabba cdecde e^3fff^3gg*; thus, it is twenty lines long.

An eighteen-line form is the HEROIC SONNET, which adds a HEROIC COUPLET to two stanzas of HEROIC OCTAVE (see the section on the RISPETTO).

A SONNET SEQUENCE is a group of sonnets on a single subject.

For other fourteen-line forms (QUATORZAINS) see the BREF DOUBLE, the SONETTO RISPETTO and the TERZA RIMA sonnet.

SPATIALS

Variously called the CALLIGRAMME, the SHAPED STANZA, or HIEROGLYPHIC VERSE, spatials may be in any form or meter. What is of importance in spatial verse is *how the poem appears on paper*: it attempts to imitate typographically a particular shape, usually one discussed in the poem itself.

Concrete verse is ideogrammic spatials. For instance. in Japanese the characters for "rain" might be arranged on the page so that it will *look* like rain falling. At the bottom of the picture there might be the character for "house"; thus, the characters for rain are falling pictorially on the character for house.

In an alphabetical language such as English concrete verse is more difficult to write and not so immediately effective. The letters of a word must be *drawn* so as to imitate the subject; i.e., the letters in the word "murder" may be drawn so as to represent a dagger.

English. Accentual-syllabic. A rhymed *stanza* of nine lines consisting of eight iambic pentameter lines and one iambic hexameter line, which is called an *Alexandrine*. The Alexandrine is always the last (ninth) line of the stanza. There is no set pattern for the rhymes.

A possible scheme:

lines:	*meters and rhymes:*				
1.	xx́	xx́	xx́	xx́	xá
2.	xx́	xx́	xx́	xx́	xb́
3.	xx́	xx́	xx́	xx́	xá
4.	xx́	xx́	xx́	xx́	xb́
5.	xx́	xx́	xx́	xx́	xb́
6.	xx́	xx́	xx́	xx́	xá
7.	xx́	xx́	xx́	xx́	xá
8.	xx́	xx́	xx́	xx́	xb́
9.	xx́	xx́	xx́	xx́	xx́	xá

For another use of the Alexandrine, see POULTER'S MEASURE.

For a form of Spenserian stanza with a set rhyme scheme, see the HUITAIN.

STAVE

English. Accentual-syllabic. Loosely, the *stanza* of a hymn or of a drinking song, both of which often utilize *refrains*. Usually, lines are tetrameter or shorter. The term may be applied more specifically to a *sestet* stanza made of three couplets and ending in a refrain: *aabbcC, ddeecC*, etc.

In a stricter version, both the first and last lines of each stave are the refrain. Thus, only the rhyme of the central couplet changes from stanza to stanza:

lines:	rhymes and refrains:
1.	A
2.	a
3.	b
4.	b
5.	a
6.	A
7.	A
8.	a
9.	c
10.	c
11.	a
12.	A
13.	etcetera.

The strict stave is a variation of the COUPLET ENVELOPE: two couplets rhyming *a* enclosing another rhyming couplet: *aabbaa*.

For other couplet forms see COUPLET, DIDACTICS, FREE VERSE, HEROICS, and POULTER'S MEASURE. For sestet forms see CLOGYRNACH, CYWYDD LLOSGYRNOG, GWAWDODYN HIR, HIR A THODDAID, RIME COUÉE, SESTET, and SHORT PARTICULAR MEASURE. See also the ENVELOPE STANZA,

A Japanese form. Syllabic. The tanka is a single QUINTET whose lines consist of five, seven, five, seven, and seven syllables respectively. It is unrhymed:

lines:	syllables:						
1.	x	x	x	x	x		
2.	x	x	x	x	x	x	x
3.	x	x	x	x	x		
4.	x	x	x	x	x	x	x
5.	x	x	x	x	x	x	x

Note that the tanka is merely a HAIKU (see TERCET) with two added lines of seven syllables each. For this reason, a separation is sometimes made between the third and fourth lines, making it a poem consisting of one TRIPLET and one COUPLET.

The idea behind a TANKA CHAIN is as follows: a haiku is written. A TANKA COUPLET is added, completing the tanka. Another haiku is added that follows logically, but that may also be read logically in place of the *first* haiku. A couplet is added completing the second tanka. A third haiku is added that may be read logically if substituted for the second haiku. A couplet is added completing the third tanka, and so on indefinitely.

TERCET

May be written in any of the meters. Any complete poem of three lines, rhymed or unrhymed.

The ENCLOSED TERCET rhymes *aba* (see enclosed TRIPLET).

The SICILIAN TERCET is an enclosed tercet written in iambic pentameter measures (see the Sicilian TRIPLET).

The TRIAD is a loose Irish form. However, a strict version consists of three tercets, each a complete poem, yet each bearing some relationship to the other two, and the whole also being interpretable as one poem. Like the other Irish forms, the triad *may* end with the first syllable, word, or line with which it began.

The *hokku* or HAIKU is a Japanese tercet. Its lines consist of five, seven, and five syllables respectively. It is unrhymed:

lines:	syllables:						
1.	x	x	x	x	x		
2.	x	x	x	x	x	x	x
3.	x	x	x	x	x		

For a form related to the *haiku* see the TANKA.

Italian. Accentual-syllabic. Any number of interlocking enclosed TRIPLET *stanzas*. The *first* and *third* lines of a stanza rhyme; the *second* line rhymes with the *first* and *third* lines of the *following* stanza. In other words, the ending of the second line of any stanza becomes the rhyme for the following stanza: *aba bcb cdc*, etc. The *poem* usually ends in a COUPLET rhymed from the second line of the last triplet: *yzy zz*. The meter is usually iambic pentameter.

Pattern:

lines:	meters and rhymes:				
1.	xx́	xx́	xx́	xx́	xá
2.	xx́	xx́	xx́	xx́	xb́
3.	xx́	xx́	xx́	xx́	xá
4.	xx́	xx́	xx́	xx́	xb́
5.	xx́	xx́	xx́	xx́	xć
6.	xx́	xx́	xx́	xx́	xb́
7.	xx́	xx́	xx́	xx́	xć
8.	xx́	xx́	xx́	xx́	xd́
9.	xx́	xx́	xx́	xx́	xć
10.	xx́	xx́	xx́	xx́	xd́
11.	xx́	xx́	xx́	xx́	xd́

The TERZA RIMA SONNET is a fourteen-line QUATORZAIN in iambic pentameter rhyming *aba bcb cdc ded ee*.

For a related form see the TERZANELLE. Another interlocking form is the interlocking RUBAIYAT. See also the MADRIGAL.

TERZANELLE

French. Syllabic. Lines may be of any length. An adaptation of TERZA RIMA to the VILLANELLE form. Nineteen lines long, composed of five interlocking enclosed TRIPLETS and a final QUATRAIN. Lines *one* and *three* reappear as refrains in the final quatrain. In addition, the middle line of each triplet is a *repeton* that reappears as the final line of the succeeding triplet, except the middle line of the last triplet, which reappears in the quatrain.

The poem may end in one of two ways, as in the diagram:

lines:	rhymes, repetons, and refrains:		
1.	A^1—*refrain*		
2.	B		
3.	A^2—*refrain*		
4.	b		
5.	C		
6.	B		
7.	c		
8.	D		
9.	C		
10.	d		
11.	E		
12.	D		
13.	e		
14.	F		
15.	E		
16.	f		
17.	A^1—*refrain*	*or*	F
18.	F		A^1—*refrain*
19.	A^2—*refrain*		A^2—*refrain*

For another form that utilizes the repeton, see the PANTOUM. Another interlocking form is the interlocking RUBAIYAT.

Welsh. Syllabic. QUATRAIN stanzas alternating between ten-syllable and nine-syllable lines. A syllable toward the end of the *first* line cross-rhymes into the middle of the *second*, and the same effect is reproduced in lines *three* and *four*. Lines *two* and *four* rhyme with each other.

The diagram:

lines:	*syllables and rhymes:*
1.	x x x x x x *a* *x* *x* *x*
2.	x x x *x* *a* *x* x x b
3.	x x x x x x *x* *x* *c* *x*
4.	x x x *c* *x* *x* x x b
5.	etcetera.

TRIOLET

A French form. Syllabic. A poem consisting of a single OCTAVE turning on two rhymes. It is built on two *refrains:* line one reappears complete as line four and again as line seven; line two reappears as line eight, completing the poem. The triolet rhymes *ABaAabAB.* Lines may be of any length.

The plot:

lines:	*refrains and rhymes:*
1.	A—*refrain*
2.	B—*refrain*
3.	a
4.	A—*refrain*
5.	a
6.	b
7.	A—*refrain*
8.	B—*refrain*

Sometimes a separation is made between lines five and six, making it a poem of two stanzas: a QUINTET and a TRIPLET.

A *stanza* consisting of three lines. It may be written in any of the meters and may be rhymed or unrhymed.

The ENCLOSED TRIPLET rhymes *aba*.

The SICILIAN TRIPLET is an enclosed triplet in iambic pentameter measures:

lines:	*meters and rhymes:*
1.	xx́ xx́ xx́ xx́ xá
2.	xx́ xx́ xx́ xx́ xb́
3.	xx́ xx́ xx́ xx́ xá
4.	etcetera.

There are two Welsh ENGLYNS that are triplet stanza forms. Both are syllabic.

ENGLYN MILWR turns on one rhyme, and each line has a count of seven syllables:

lines:	*syllables and rhymes:*
1.	x x x x x x a
2.	x x x x x x a
3.	x x x x x x a
4.	etcetera.

ENGLYN PENFYR is a stanza whose lines consist respectively of ten, seven, and seven syllables rhyming *AAA*. One, two, *or* three syllables occur at the end of the *first* line *after* the *main* rhyme. These syllables are *echoed* by assonance, alliteration, *or* secondary rhyme in the *first few* syllables of the *second* line. The main rhyme *ends* the second and third lines:

lines:	*syllables and rhymes:*
1.	x x x x x x x x x A *b*
2.	*b x x* x x x A
3.	x x x x x x A

4.	x x x x x x x C x x d
5.	x d x x x x x C
6.	x x x x x x C
7.	x x x x x x x x E x f
8.	f x x x x x x E
9.	x x x x x x E
10.	etcetera.

For set forms and uses of the triplet or enclosed triplet also see the sections on the TERCET, TERZA RIMA, TERZA-NELLE, TRIVERSEN, and VILLANELLE.

This is a native form. It, and variations of it, have been appearing in American verse with some regularity during the twentieth century, but it is here isolated and named for the first time.

It is written in either accentual or accentual-syllabic measures. The triversen is eighteen lines long and is composed of six *end-stopped* TRIPLETS. Each line equals approximately one phrase, and each triplet equals one clause. In each line there are generally *no more* than four and *no less* than two accented syllables. Otherwise, lines may be of any length. The poem may be rhymed or unrhymed.

In the case of the metrical version, read *verse feet* for "accented syllables."

A possible scheme in accentuals:

lines:	*words, accents, syllables, sentences:*
1.	x́ xx́ x xx́x xx x́
2.	xx́ xxx́ x x́
3.	xxx́ x x́x.—*end 1st sentence*
4.	etcetera for 18 lines: 6 end–stopped triplets, each of which is one sentence or clause.

A somewhat similar form is the TRIAD, which will be found in the section on the TERCET.

For an explanation of the general prosody (sometimes called "projective verse") behind the triversen, see *variable foot*.

Most forms may be utilized as vehicles for narration or *story-telling*. However, certain forms traditionally serve this function, particularly the BALLAD, EPIC, FABLIAU, LAY, and ROMANCE, all of which are dealt with elsewhere in this book. However, the three major forms might be ranked and defined thus:

I. EPIC: A long, heroic verse narrative.
II. ROMANCE: A long, lyric verse narrative.
III. BALLAD: A relatively short, lyric verse narrative.

The two minor forms might be defined, very loosely, in this way:

IV. FABLIAU: A short-story in rhymed verse.
V. LAY: A vignette in song form.

See the sections on the BALLAD and related forms. For further information about the epic, see the section concerned with HEROICS; for the lay and romance, see the LYRICS section; for the *fabliau*, see SATIRICS.

A French form. Syllabic. Lines may be of any length. Nineteen lines divided into six stanzas—five TRIPLETS and one QUATRAIN—turning on two rhymes and built on two refrains. The refrains consist of lines one and three complete. Line one reappears as lines six, twelve, and eighteen; line three reappears as lines nine, fifteen, and nineteen, finishing the poem. The rhyme scheme is A^1bA^2 abA^1 abA^2 abA^1 abA^2 abA^1A^2:

lines:	refrains and rhymes:
1.	A^1—*refrain*
2.	b
3.	A^2—*refrain*
4.	a
5.	b
6.	A^1—*refrain*
7.	a
8.	b
9.	A^2—*refrain*
10.	a
11.	b
12.	A^1—*refrain*
13.	a
14.	b
15.	A^2—*refrain*
16.	a
17.	b
18.	A^1—*refrain*
19.	A^2—*refrain*

Bibliography of Examples:

A List of Recommended *Contemporary* Poems
Written in the Various Forms,
and Variations of the Forms.

ACROSTIC: "Song Made in Lieu of Other Ornaments" by Spencer Brown, in *Poets of Today III*, ed. Wheelock (Charles Scribner's Sons, 1956); "Knife Is the Name: To Write in Less than Blood," "Jacks and Jills Who Find the Day's Eyes Gone" in *The Sorrows of Cold Stone*, by John Malcolm Brinnin (Dodd, Mead and Co., 1951); "Flights" in *The Lovemaker*, by Robert Mezey (Cummington Press, 1961).

ANGLO-SAXON PROSODY: "The Coming of Robin Hood," Section V of "A Little Geste" in *A Little Geste*, by Daniel G. Hoffman (Oxford University Press, 1960).

BALLAD: "Dick Dongworth on the Death of Roseblush" in *A Crackling of Thorns*, by John Hollander (Yale University Press, 1958); "The Ballad of Red Fox" in *The Clever Body*, by Melvin Walker LaFollette (Spenserian Press, 1959); "The Good Man" in *Walls and Distances*, by David Galler (The Macmillan Co., 1959); "An Immigrant Ballad" in *First Poems*, by Lewis Turco (Golden Quill Press, 1960).

BALLAD STANZA: "The Man in the Man-Made Moon" in *Nude Descending a Staircase*, by X. J. Kennedy (Doubleday & Co., 1961).

BALLADE: "Ballade of the Inventory: In Provence" in *Light and Dark*, by Barbara Howes (Wesleyan University Press, 1959); "Ballade for Braque" in *Coming of Age*, by Babette Deutsch (Indiana University Press, 1959); "Mother of the Saint" in *The Love Letters of Phyllis McGinley* (Viking Press, 1954); "Ballade of Blind Alleys" by Vassar Miller, in *The New Orleans Poetry Journal*, Vol. I, no. 4, 1955; "Ballade of the Session after Camillo," by David Galler, *Walls and Distances*, *op. cit.*

BLANK VERSE: "The Fishermen" in *Green with Beasts*, by W. S. Merwin (London: Rupert Hart-Davis, 1956); "A Gloomy Looking Man" in *The Pageless Air*, by Ralph L. Kinsey (Golden Quill Press, 1959); "The Death of Venus" in *The Death of Venus, and Others*, by Harold Witt (Golden Quill Press, 1958).

CHANT ROYAL: "The Old Professor," by Lewis Turco, *First Poems*, *op. cit.*

CINQUAIN: "The Soul" by Babette Deutsch, *Coming of Age*, *op. cit.*; "St. John, Baptist," "St. Sebastian," "St. Francis of Assisi" by Melvin Walker La Follette, *The Clever Body*, *op. cit.*

COMMON MEASURE: "Totentanz" by Lewis Turco, (untitled first poem in) *First Poems*, *op. cit.*

COUPLET: "The Wisdom of Insecurity" in *Great Praises*, by Richard Eberhart (Oxford University Press, 1957); "The Drunken Fisherman" in *Lord Weary's Castle*, by Robert Lowell (Harcourt, Brace, 1961).

CYHYDEDD FER: "Exclusive Blue" in *The Orb Weaver*, by Robert Francis (Wesleyan University Press, 1960); "Cormorants" in *Colonel Johnson's Ride*, by Robert Huff (Wayne State University Press, 1958); "The House and the Tree," by Spencer Brown, *Poets of Today III*, *op. cit.*

CYWYDD LLOSGYRNOG: "Where Once the Waters of Your Face" in *Collected Poems*, by Dylan Thomas (New Directions Books, 1953).

ENGLYNS and ALL OTHER WELSH FORMS: Various poems in *Green Armor on Green Ground*, by Rolfe Humphries (Charles Scribner's Sons, 1956).

ENGLYN UNODL CRWCA: "On a Wedding Anniversary" by Dylan Thomas, *Collected Poems*, *op. cit.*

EPIGRAM: "Palaver's No Prayer" in 39 *Poems*, by John Ciardi (Rutgers University Press, 1959); various poems in *The Exclusions of a Rhyme*, by J. V. Cunningham (Alan Swallow, 1960).

EPITAPH: "Epitaph for Our Landlord" in *Portrait of Your Niece*, by Carol Hall (University of Minnesota Press, 1959); "Epitaph" by Robert Francis, *The Orb Weaver*, *op. cit.*; "Little Elegy," "Epitaph for a Postal Clerk" by X. J. Kennedy, *Nude Descending a Staircase*, *op. cit.*

GLOSE: "Homage to J. S. Bach" in *The Crow and the Heart*, by Hayden Carruth (The Macmillan Co., 1959).

HAIKU: "Haiku: A Seasonal Sequence" by Clara M. Cassidy, in *Japan: Theme & Variations*, ed. Tuttle (Chas. E. Tuttle Co., 1959).

HENDECASYLLABICS: "Hendecasyllabics" by John Hollander, in *Fine Arts Magazine* (University of Connecticut), Vol. IV, no. 1, 1959.

HEROIC COUPLET: "It Is June, This Jesting Heat" by Robert Mezey, *The Lovemaker*, *op. cit.*; "Andromeda" by Graham Hough, in *Poetry 1960—An Appetiser*, a supplement of *The Critical Quarterly*, 1960.

KYRIELLE: "Sunday Psalm" by Phyllis McGinley, *The Love Letters*, *op. cit.*; "Dinky" in *Words for the Wind*, by Theodore Roethke (Doubleday & Co., 1958).

MADSONG: "Odds Bodkin's Springsong" by Lewis Turco in *Red Clay Reader 3*, 1966; "The Song of Mad Tom's Dog," in *Songs*, by Christopher Logue (McDowell-Obolensky, 1959).

NASHERS: Many poems by Ogden Nash in his various books.

OCTAVE: "Improvising" in *The World's One Clock*, by Louise Townsend Nicholl (St. Martin's Press, 1959); "Coffee-House Lecture" by Robert Mezey in *The Lovemaker*, *op. cit.*; "A Song for the Middle of the Night" in *The Green Wall*, by James Wright (Yale University Press, 1957).

ODE: "Summer: University Town" in *The Gazebos* by Edwin Honig (Clarke & Way, Inc., 1959); "Necromanteion" by Lewis Turco in *The Carolina Quarterly*, Vol. XVI, no. 1, 1963, and "Ode for the Beat Generation" by the same author in *First Poems*, *op. cit.*

OTTAVA RIMA: "Flag Day 1954," "The Spy to the Hero"

in *Last Poems*, by Edgar Bogardus (Kenyon Review Press, 1960).

QUATRAIN: "On a Photograph of My Grandfather" in *The Broken Frieze*, by Peter Everwine (Hillside Press, 1958); "I, the Childless One" in *Collected Poems*, by George Abbe (Richard R. Smith, 1961); "A Mad Negro Soldier Confined at Munich" in *Life Studies*, by Robert Lowell (Farrar, Straus & Cudahy, 1959); "The Lecturer Orders His Notes" in *The Walks Near Athens*, by Hollis Summers (Harper & Bros., 1959).

QUINTET: "The Black Swan" in *The Seven-League Crutches*, by Randall Jarrell (Harcourt, Brace & Co., 1951); "The Young Girl of the Mississippi Valley" in *Body of Waking*, by Muriel Rukeyser (Harper & Bros., 1958); "Seminary" in *The Middle Voice*, by Constance Carrier (Alan Swallow, 1955); "Poem Written in Late Autumn" by Albert Herzing in *Poets of Today VIII*, *op. cit.*

RANNAIGHEACHT GHAIRID: "Pocoangelini 3" by Lewis Turco in *Poetry*, Vol. 108, No. 3, July, 1966.

RIME ROYAL: "Beside My Grandmother" by Alfred M. Lee in *Midland*, ed. Engle (Random House, 1961): "Thoughts from the Boston Post Road" by Lewis Turco in *First Poems*, *op. cit.*

RISPETTO: "I Have No Praises" by David R. Slavitt in *Poets of Today VIII*, *op. cit.*; "Exeunt" in *Things of this World*, by Richard Wilbur (Harcourt, Brace & Co., 1956); "Blue Jay" by Robert Francis in *The Orb Weaver*, *op. cit.*; "Good Boy" by William Stafford in *A Houyhnhnm's Scrapbook*, no. 2, February, 1957; "The Voyage" in *Lupercal*, by Ted Hughes (Harper & Bros., 1960); "Although I Remember the Sound" by Robert Huff in *Colonel Johnson's Ride*, *op. cit.*

RONDEAU: "Death of a Vermont Farm Woman" by Barbara Howes in *Light and Dark*, *op. cit.*; "A Long Time Ago" by Nicholas Moore in *Poetry Quarterly* (England), Summer, 1950.

RONDEL: "Rondeau" by X. J. Kennedy in *Nude Descending*

a Staircase, op. cit.; "Rondel" in *Survivor's Leave* by Charles Causley, Aldington, Kent, England: Hand and Flower Press, 1953.

SAPPHICS: "Heart of Snow" by John Hollander in *A Crackling of Thorns, op. cit.*; "Legend for a Shield" in *Poems*, by Richmond Lattimore (University of Michigan Press, 1957); "Visitor" by Lewis Turco in *First Poems, op. cit.*; "Erinna to Sappho" by John Hollander in *A Crackling of Thorns, op. cit.*; "I Am Disquieted When I See Many Hills" in *Apples from Shinar*, by Hyam Plutzik (Wesleyan University Press, 1959).

SEPTET: "Here Come the Saints" in *Fighting Terms*, by Thom Gunn (Hawk's Well Press, 1958); "For a Friend Getting Married" in *Depth of Meaning*, by Christopher Wiseman (Iowa City: privately printed, 1960); "Lullaby" by James Scully in *Poetry* (Chicago), December, 1961; "Cages" in *Light in the West*, by Judson Jerome (Golden Quill Press, 1962).

SESTET: "April Inventory" in *Heart's Needle*, by W.D. Snodgrass (Alfred A. Knopf, Inc., 1959); "An End to No Encounter" by Norman Friedman in *Fine Arts Magazine* (University of Connecticut), Vol. III, no. 1, 1958; "Counting the Mad" in *The Summer Anniversaries*, by Donald Justice (Wesleyan University Press, 1960); "Autumnal Spring Song" by Vassar Miller in *New Orleans Poetry Journal*, Vol. I, no. 4, 1955.

SESTINA: "Sestina" in *On the Morning of Color*, by John Woods (Indiana University Press, 1961); "Sestina" in *The Aging Ghost*, by James Crenner (Golden Quill Press, 1964); "*Étude*: Andantino" in *Of the Festivity*, by William Dickey (Yale University Press, 1959); "A Dream Sestina" by Donald Justice in *The Summer Anniversaries, op. cit.*

SICILIAN OCTAVE: "The Widow's Rape" by Lewis Turco in *The Carolina Quarterly*, Vol. XVI, no. 1, 1963; "Daphne" by Fay Fox in *The Fenn Literary Omnibus*, Vol. I, 1963.

SKELTONICS: "Odds Bodkin's Strange Thrusts and Ravels" (a long satire on contemporary poetry) by Lewis Turco in

The Oberlin Quarterly, Part I: Vol. I, no. 1, 1963; Part II: Vol. I, no. 2, 1964.

SONNET: "Woman at the Window" in *The Wilderness and Other Poems* by Louis O. Coxe (University of Minnesota Press, 1958); "The Beautiful American Word, Sure" in *Summer Knowledge*, by Delmore Schwartz, (Doubleday & Co., Inc., 1959); "A Summer Idyll" in *The Self-Made Man*, by Reed Whittemore (The Macmillan Co., 1959); "Sonnet I" from "The Name of Love" in *Poems in Praise* by Paul Engle (Random House, 1959); "The City Considered as a Tulip Tree" in *The Man Behind You*, by Carl Bode (E. P. Dutton & Co., Inc., 1960); "Double Sonnet" in *A Summoning of Stones*, by Anthony Hecht (The Macmillan Co., 1954).

SPATIALS: "Mirror Image: Port-au-Prince" by Barbara Howes in *Light and Dark*, *op. cit.*; "Mirror," "Pendulum" in *The Carpentered Hen*, by John Updike (Harper & Bros., 1958); "400-Meter Free-Style" in *Halfway*, by Maxine W. Kumin (Holt, Rhineart, & Winston, 1961); "Totem" in *The Fortune Teller*, by John Holmes (Harper & Bros., 1961).

SPENSERIAN STANZA: "The Tandem Ride" in *Madonna of the Cello*, by Robert Bagg (Wesleyan University Press, 1961).

SPLIT COUPLET: "Two Octobers" by Richmond Lattimore in *Poems*, *op. cit.*; "Two Wrestlers" by Robert Francis in *The Orb Weaver*, *op. cit.*

STAVE: "Song for Strangers in Wales" in *Selected Poems* by John Malcolm Brinnin (Atlantic-Little, Brown, 1963).

TANKA: "After Masako" by Harriet Winnick in *Japan: Theme & Variations*, *op. cit.*

TERCET: "On the Calculus" by J. V. Cunningham in *The Exclusions of a Rhyme*, *op. cit.*; "Epitaph for Some Poet or Other" by Hayden Carruth in *The Crow and the Heart*, *op. cit.*; "Nutcracker" by John Updike in *The Carpentered Hen*, *op. cit.*

TERZA RIMA: "Home to Ostia" by G. F. Keithley in *The*

Wormwood Review, Vol. I, no. 2, 1960; "Admission of Guilt" in *Letter from a Distant Land*, by Philip Booth (Viking Press, 1957); "On a Certain Engagement South of Seoul" by Hayden Carruth in *The Crow and the Heart*, *op. cit.*; "Plato's Cave: The Annex" in *Mosaic*, by Frederic Will (Pennsylvania State University Press, 1959); "Meeting" in *The Hawk in the Rain*, by Ted Hughes (Harper & Bros., 1957).

TRIOLET: "Triolet" by Louise Townsend Nicholl in *The World's One Clock*, *op. cit.*; "Insight," "Wind-Song" in *Poems*, by Diane Musser (Theo. Gauss' Sons, Inc., 1958).

TRIPLET: "Harlowe Young" in *Aspects of Proteus*, by Hyam Plutzik (Harper & Bros., 1949); "Any Object" by May Swenson in *Poets of Today I*, ed. Wheelock (Chas. Scribner's Sons, 1954); "Scratch" from "The Wandering Jew" in *Works and Days*, by Irving Feldman (Atlantic-Little, Brown, 1961).

TRIVERSEN: "Words from England" in *Exiles and Marriages*, by Donald Hall (The Viking Press, 1955); "The Movement of the Worlds" by Kenneth McRobbie in *Poetry*, Vol. 96, no. 3, June, 1960; "Address" by Hayden Carruth in *The Crow and the Heart*, *op. cit.*; "Monday's Vision" in *Testament and Other Poems*, by John Fandel (Sheed & Ward, 1959); "Mulling It Over" by James Crenner in *The Aging Ghost*, *op. cit.*; "Six Sections of a Mask" by Lewis Turco in *First Poems*, *op. cit.*

VILLANELLE: "Do Not Go Gentle into That Good Night" by Dylan Thomas in *Collected Poems*, *op. cit.*; "Beyond Surprise" in *The Colours of Memory* by George Reavey (Grove Press, 1955); "Lament" by Sylvia Plath in *The New Orleans Poetry Journal*, Vol. I, no. 4, 1955; "Villanelle" by Weldon Kees in *Collected Poems*, *op. cit.*; "Women in Love" by Donald Justice in *The Summer Anniversaries*, *op. cit.*; "The Waking" by Theodore Roethke in *Words for the Wind*, *op. cit.*

Glossarial Index

antistrophe, 84

ANTITHETICAL PARALLELISM, 70

antonyms: words that have opposite meanings.

aphorism, 63

apocopated rhyme, 25

aposiopesis, 29

apostrophe, 29

approximate rhyme—see *off-rhyme.*

Arabic forms, 59, 106–107

archaism: a word or locution that is no longer to be found in normal contemporary speech; a linguistic anachronism.

archetype: seminal or original source; prototype.

architectonics—see *fusional level.*

argument—see *ideational level.*

arsis—see *unaccented syllable.*

association—see *connotation.*

assonance, 19–20, 25

AUBADE—see ALBA.

Augustan—see *neoclassical,* esp. entry 2.

AWDL GYWYDD, 45

BALLAD, 46, 131

BALLAD STANZA, 46

BALLADE, 47–48

BALLADE À DOUBLE REFRAIN, 48

BALLADE SUPRÊME, 47

bard, 18

baroque: an artistic and literary style of the seventeenth century characterized by fantastic and grotesque imagery and complexity of form.

beat—see *accent.*

beat poets: a school of poets that came to prominence in the 1950's. They were characterized by verse that was rhetorical and didactic. The content of their work was largely concerned with social criticism, and they used a variety of free-verse forms, but particularly the loose Biblical parallelisms of Whitman and the Imagist patterns of W.C. Williams and the early Ezra Pound.

bibliography of examples, 133–139

BLANK VERSE, 49

BOB—see BOB AND WHEEL.

BOB AND WHEEL, 50

breath pause, 69

BREF DOUBLE, 51

breve, 15

broken rhyme—see *apocopated rhyme*.

BUCOLIC—see ECLOGUE and PASTORAL.

burden, 26, 46

BURNS STANZA—see STANDARD HABBIE

BYR A THODDAID, 52

cacophony, 25

cadence—see *rhythm*.

caesura, 18, 20, 22, 44, 89

CALLIGRAMME—see SPATIALS.

Calliope—see *Muse*.

CANSO, 80

CANTICLE, 80

canto: a major sub-unit of a long poem; a verse chapter.

CANZO—see CANSO.

CANZONE—see CANSO.

carmen figuratum—see SPATIALS.

CAROL, 53

Caroline: the period of Charles I of England, 1625–49.

carpe diem motif: the "seize the day" convention of living the present moment to the fullest.

CASBAIRDNE, 54

catalexis, 23

CAUDATED SONNET, 117

cavalier poets: aristocratic poets of the *Caroline* period. See *Caroline*.

Celtic forms, 42; see also *Irish forms*, *Welsh forms*.

Chanson de Geste: a type of medieval French EPIC with marked lyric qualities.

CHANT, 80

CHANTEY, 80

CHANT ROYAL, 55

CHAUCERIAN STANZA—see RIME ROYAL.

CHORIAMBICS, 56

CINQUAIN, 56

classical: formal in structure, traditional in treatment; characteristic of Greek or Roman systems: objective rather than subjective, restrained rather than emotional. Clarity and simplicity of style are important features of classicism. Concerned with society, morals, manners, reason, common sense.

CLASSICAL HEXAMETER, 65

CLASSICAL PENTAMETER, 65

classical prosody—see *quantitative verse*.

CLERIHEW, 11

cliché: a trite expression.

diphthongs, 23, 66

dipodics: an accentual prosody standing halfway between Anglo-Saxon prosody and metrical verse. Many nursery rhymes are dipodic, as is much of the work of John Crowe Ransom and Theodore Roethke.

The dipodic line, like a hemistich of Anglo-Saxon prosody, contains two stresses; the first is a light (or secondary), stress, the second stress is heavy. However, in certain instances this pattern may be reversed. Normally, two dipodic lines form a half-unit, and two more lines are needed to complete the unit, which is rhymed; often the rhymes used are feminine:

> Òld Mother Goóse,
> When she wànted to wánder,
> Róde through the áir
> On a vèry fine gánder.

In effect, every two dipodic lines is a stich of Anglo-Saxon prosody divided by a caesura, and the four dipodic lines equal a couplet of rhymed Anglo-Saxon prosody (with or without alliteration):

> Òld Mother Goóse, · When she wànted to wánder,
> Róde through the áir · On a vèry fine gánder . . . ,

and sometimes the lines are written out in just such fashion:

> There wàs an old wóman · who lìved in a shóe.
> She had só many chìldren · she dìdn't know whát to do.

For a related form, see *Skeltonics*. See also *sprung rhythm*.

dipody, 63

direct address—see *apostrophe*.

DIRGE—see ELEGY.

dispersion: a technique of e.e. cummings and others. A poem is first written in a traditional form. The poem's form is then disguised, or "dispersed," according to some pattern other than its original line or stanza structure, such as by phrase units, by halving the lines, by breaking lines at *caesuras*, or by running two or more lines together.

dissociation of sensibility—see *sensibility*.

dissonance, 25

distich—see *couplet*.

distributed stress: a situation that occurs when there is uncertainty concerning which of two consecutive syllables is to be accented. See *spondee*.

disyllabic: comprised of two syllables.

DITHYRAMB, 80

division, 15

DIZAIN, 48

DOGGEREL, 80, 109

DOUBLE ACROSTIC, 41

DOUBLE BALLADE, 47–48

DOUBLE BALLADE SUPRÊME, 47–48

double rhymes, 25, 42

DRAMATIC MONOLOGUE—see MONOLOGUE.

DRAMATICS, 63

dream vision: a convention wherein the poet falls asleep and has a dream, which he narrates.

DROIGHNEACH, 64

dunadh, 42

ECLOGUE, 63, 81

Edwardians: a school of poets in England at the turn of the twentieth century.

eighteen-line forms, 37

eight-line forms, 36

ELEGIACS, 65

ELEGY, 80

eleven-line forms, 37

elision, 18, 22–23. See also *synalepha* and *syncope*.

ellipsis, 30

emblem, 29

embryonic rhyme—see *off-rhyme*.

ENCLOSED TERCET, 123

ENCLOSED TRIPLET, 128

encomiastic: written in praise of. See ODE.

end-stop, 22

end-words, 113–114.

English forms, 44, 50, 53, 74, 79, 80–81, 82, 84–85, 89, 105, 109, 116–118, 120, 121

ENGLISH ODE, 84–85

ENGLISH SONNET, 116–117

ENGLYN CYRCH, 66

ENGLYN LLEDDFBROEST, 66

ENGLYN MILWR, 128

ENGLYN PENFYR, 128–129

ENGLYN PROEST DALGRON, 66

ENGLYN PROEST GADWYNOG, 67

ENGLYNS, 66–67, 128–129

ENGLYN UNODL CRWCA, 67

ENGLYN UNODL UNION, 67

enjambment, 18, 22

French forms, 47–48, 51, 53, 55, 75–79, 97, 100–104, 109, 113–114, 117, 125, 127, 131, 132

fusional level, 21

Georgians: a British school of poetry of the time of King George V of England.

GEORGICS, 63

GLOSE, 71

gnomic verse—see *aphorism*.

Gongorism: an affected style of writing similar to *euphuism*. After Luis de Góngora y Argote, Spanish poet, 1571–1627.

grammatics, 70

gratuitous metaphor—see *metaphoric construction*.

greater Ionic—see *Ionic*.

Greek forms, 43, 56, 65, 74, 80–81, 84

GWAWDODYN, 73

GWAWDODYN HIR, 73

GWAWDODYNS, 73

HAIKU, 123

half-rhyme—see *off-rhyme*.

hangers—see *outrides*.

head rhyme, 24

Hebrew prosody, 70

hemistich, 44, 89

HENDECASYLLABICS, 74

heptameter, 17

HEROIC COUPLET, 74

HEROIC LINE, 74

HEROIC OCTAVE, 99

HEROIC RISPETTO, 99

HEROICS, 74, 91, 99, 117

HEROIC SONNET, 117

HEROIC STANZA, 74, 91

HEROIC VERSE—see HEROICS.

hexameter, 17

hexasyllabic: comprised of six syllables.

HIEROGLYPHIC VERSE—see SPATIALS.

HIR A THODDAID, 75

HOKKU—see HAIKU.

hold—see *pause*.

homograph—see *homonyms*.

homonyms: words spelled alike, but having different meanings.

homophone—see *homonyms*.

HOMOSTROPHIC ODE, 84

Malayan form, 88

masculine ending, 24, 108

masculine rhyme, 24

measures—see *verse feet*.

meiosis—see *irony*.

melopoieia—see LYRICS.

metaphor, 27. See also *metaphoric construction*.

metaphoric construction: the *vehicle* of a metaphor is the *figure of speech* that is used to bear the weight of the comparison of two dissimilar things or qualities that have a single point in common. The *tenor* is the subject of the metaphor. A *gratuitous metaphor* is one that does not spring "naturally" from the context of the poem, whereas an *organic metaphor* is one that does. A *mixed metaphor* is one whose vehicle is inappropriate to the tenor, or the vehicle itself is made up of inappropriate elements or a combination of disparate elements, i.e., "keep your nose to the grindstone and your ear to the ground." A *subdued metaphor* is a metaphor that is *implied* by the context of the poem, not stated.

metaphysical poetry, 27

meter, 15–20

metonymy, 30

metrical notation, 19–20, 46

METRICAL ROMANCE—see ROMANCE.

metrical tail—see BOB AND WHEEL.

metrical unit, 15–17

metrical variation, 17, 21–23

metrics, 15–20

minnesinger—see *minstrel*.

minstrel: see *troubadour*, for which minstrel is *not* a synonym.

mixed metaphor—see *metaphoric construction*.

mock-forms, 109

mode—prose or verse. See also *poet* and 109.

MONK'S TALE STANZA— see HUITAIN.

MONODY—see ELEGY.

MONOLOGUE, 63

monometer, 17

mora—see *breve*.

MOTE, 82

motif—see *archetype*, *carpe diem*, *ubi sunt*.

Muse: in classical mythology, a goddess of poetry; *Calliope* was the Muse of epic poetry, *Euterpe* of lyric poetry, *Erato* of love poetry, and *Polyhymnia* of sacred poetry. The term *muse* may apply also to the personal genius of a poet. (The name of this Author's Muse is *Jascha*.)

mythopoesis: myth-making.

mythopoet: a poet who in his work practices *mythopoeia*.

narrative, 46, 131

narrative forms—see VERSE NARRATIVES.

NASHERS, 69

near-rhyme—see *off-rhyme*.

neoclassical: 1) contemporary or modern, but having the qualities associated with classical poetry; 2) English poetry of the eighteenth century: *Augustan*.

neologism: a coined or newly invented word.

nine-line forms, 36

nineteen-line forms, 38

ninety-eight-line forms, 38

nonasyllabic: comprised of nine syllables.

nonsense verse, 79, 80, 109

normative meter, 17–18

numbers—see *meter* and *metrics*.

NURSERY RHYME, 80

objective: without emotional involvement; dispassionate, analytical.

objective correlative—see *concretion* and *sensory pattern*.

oblique rhyme—see *off-rhyme*.

occasional poetry: verse composed in commemoration. See particularly the ODE and the ELEGY.

OCTAVE, 83

octave forms, 36

octosyllabic: comprised of eight syllables.

ODE, 80, 84–85

off-rhyme, 19, 25

OMAR STANZA—see RUBAI.

one-line forms, 32–33

onomatopoeia, 29

open couplet—see *enjambment*.

orchestration, 28, 30

organic metaphor—see *metaphoric construction*.

OTTAVA RIMA, 86

outrides—Gerard Manley Hopkins's term for the unaccented syllables in accentual verse.

oxymoron, 28

paeon: any one of four metrical feet; each is composed of four syllables one stressed and three unstressed: –ᴜᴜᴜ, ᴜ–ᴜᴜ, ᴜᴜ–ᴜ, ᴜᴜᴜ–.

palindrome: any language unit that reads the same backward or forward.

PALINODE, 87

paranomasia—see *pun*.

paraphones—see *off-rhyme*.

pararhyme—see *off-rhyme*.

Parnassian poetry: poetry of a second order written by poets of a first order.

Parnassian poets: a mid-nineteenth-century school of French poetry.

Parnassus: the mountain sacred to Apollo and the Muses, symbolic of poetry in particular and the arts in general.

parody: caricature of a well-known literary work. A satiric mode.

PASTORAL, 80–81

PASTORAL ELEGY, 81

pathetic fallacy: as distinguished from *personification*, which is a form of metaphor, pathetic fallacy is the endowment of inanimate or subhuman objects with absurdly human characteristics, i.e., "The little white cloud that cried."

pattern, 21; see also *forms*.

patterned verse—see SPATIALS.

pause—see *caesura, end-stop*, and *phrasing*.

PEARLINE STANZA, 89

Pegasus: a winged horse of Greek mythology. With a blow of his hoof he caused Hippocrene, the fountain of poetic inspiration, to spring from Mount Helicon; symbolic of poetic inspiration.

pentasyllabic: comprised of five syllables.

periphrasis, 30

personification, 29

PETRARCHAN SONNET—see ITALIAN SONNET.

phanopoeia—see *image, sensory pattern*.

phrasing, 22, 69–70, 130. See also *projective verse* and *variable foot*.

PINDARIC ODE, 84

poem: an artifice of language. See *poet*. See also p. 21.

poem forms, 41, 46, 47–48, 51, 53, 55, 56, 63, 69–70, 71, 74, 75, 76–78, 79, 80–81, 82, 84–85, 87, 88, 91, 92, 99, 100–102, 103, 104, 105, 106–107, 108, 109, 111, 112, 113–114, 116–118, 119, 121, 122, 123, 125, 127, 130, 131, 132

poesy; poetry—see *poem*.

poet: an artificer of language, as distinguished from the fictionist, who is an artificer of written narrative; the dramatist, who is an artificer of theatrical narrative; and the essayist, who is an artificer of rhetorical exposition. The poet is a writer whose focus is primarily on the language itself; the fictionist and dramatist concentrate upon the story-line, the essayist concentrates upon the examination of a subject. Thus, poetry is not determined by a particular mode, such as verse, for even prose may be utilized to concentrate upon language (see FREE VERSE).

The distinction, then, is not between poetry and prose, but between poetry and fiction; poetry and drama; poetry and essay. Thus, fiction may be written in verse and still be fiction, not poetry (if the concentration is upon the story-line rather than upon the language); plays may be written in verse, and essays in verse, and still be plays or essays. See also *bard* and *maker*.

poetaster: an unskilled dabbler in versification.

poetic: partaking of the qualities associated with poetry.

poetic diction: as opposed to intensified normal speech, poetic diction is contrived of speech forms invented for the purpose of verse composition.

poetic justice: punishment, administered by the gods (evidently with the counsel of the Muses), to fit the crime.

poetic license: a document issued by the Anti-Muses to poetasters. Allegedly, this license gives its holder the right to do anything he pleases in verse, and to call the results poetry; however, the poetic license owns many of the characteristics of Confederate Money.

poetics—see *prosody*.

poet laureate: 1) an academic degree; 2) an official title.

poetry—see *poem, poet*. Any writing which successfully focuses on language.

Polyhymnia—see *Muse*.

polyphonic prose, 69

Portuguese forms, 71–72

POULTER'S MEASURE, 90

primary accent—see *ictus*.

PRIMER COUPLET, 63

projective verse: essentially, a prosody based partly upon a system of variable accentuals (see *variable foot*), and partly upon a system of *grammatics*. See *breath pause, parallelism, phrasing*, TRIVERSEN, *verse paragraph, verse sentence*.

PROSE POEM, 69

prosodic symbols, 15–20

prosodic systems—see *prosody*.

prosody, 15–20, 68–70

prosopopoeia—see *personification*.

PROTHALAMION, 80

pun, 27

pure poetry: poetry written simply on the level of *euphony* and without any larger intention to instruct, moralize, or edify.

pyrrhic, 15

QASĪDA, 59

quality, 18, 21

quantitative verse, 15

quantity, 18, 21

running rhythm—see *normative meter*.
run-on lines—see *enjambment*.
scald: in ancient times, a Scandinavian *bard*.
scansion, 16–17
Scottish forms, 97. See also BALLAD.
secondary accent, 15–16, See also *dipodics*.
secondary rhyme, 52
semi-vowels, 22–23
sensibility: sensitiveness. T. S. Eliot and others have maintained that creative sensibility is composed of two parts: the intellect and the emotions. If, in a poet, one is dissociated from the other, there is a *dissociation of sensibility*, and poetic imbalance may occur: on the one hand, poetry that is too much "of the mind" may be written; on the other, there may be poetry too much "of the emotions."
sensory level, 21
septasyllabic: comprised of seven syllables.
SEPTENARY—see FOURTEENER.
SEPTET, 111
septet forms, 36
SERENADE, 81
SESTET, 112
sestet forms, 35–36
SESTINA, 113–114
seven-line forms, 36
SEXTILLA, 112
SHAKESPEARIAN SONNET—see ENGLISH SONNET.
SHAPED STANZA—see SPATIALS.

sprung rhythm: Gerard Manley Hopkins's term for the accentual rhythms that are to be found in *Anglo-Saxon prosody*, *dipodics*, and *Skeltonics*. The difference is that the term "sprung rhythm" is descriptive of the general accentual prosody that includes all three forms.

    Anglo-Saxon prosody, dipodics, and Skeltonics utilize accents that are made all the heavier by means of alliteration or substitution. The first case is explained in the sections dealing with the three forms named, and in the chapter on *Metrics*.

In the case of *substitution*, Hopkins points out that sprung rhythm arises when a reverse foot is substituted for a foot of the running rhythm (or *normative meter*) of a poem (i.e., a dactyl for an iamb in an iambic poem). He distinguishes between the "alliterative" sprung rhythm and the "substitutive" sprung rhythm by pointing out that the latter is *counterpoint*: ". . . the super-inducing or *mounting* of a new rhythm upon the old [normative]; and since the new or mounted rhythm is actually heard and at the same time the mind naturally supplies the [normative] rhythm . . . , two rhythms are. . . running at once and we have something answerable to counterpoint in music." This same point is made in simpler language in the chapter on *Metrics* and elsewhere in *The Book of Forms*. For Hopkins's detailed theory one may consult the "Author's Preface" to the *Poems* (1876–1889).

In a poem written in sprung rhythm, other than in the three forms named, the number of accents of each line is determined by the author.

An accentual system that is not a part of the sprung-rhythm theory is the American *variable foot* prosody of William Carlos Williams. Williams's invention is not dependent upon alliteration or substitution.

suspended rhyme—see *consonance*.

syllabic forms, 42, 45, 47–48, 51, 52, 54, 55, 56, 57, 60, 61, 62, 64, 66–67, 73, 75, 76–78, 93–94, 95–96, 97, 98, 100–102, 103, 104, 109, 110, 112, 113–114, 115, 122, 123, 125, 126, 127, 128–129, 132

syllabic verse, 16, 18

symbol, 29

symbolist: a poet whose work operates on the level of *symbol*.

sympathy: a state in which one's emotions are involved in the situation or state of another person.

synaeresis—see *synalepha*.

synalepha: a technique of overt *elision* by means of which one of two adjacent unaccented syllables is suppressed in order to achieve the effect of only one unaccented syllable; i.e., "Th' art of poetic diction." See *vowels*.

syncopation—see *counterpoint*.

syncope—see *semi-vowels*.

synechdoche, 30

synesthesia, 29

SYNONYMOUS PARALLELISM, 70

synonyms: words having the same meanings.

SYNTHETIC PARALLELISM, 70

tact: the choices the poet must make as he proceeds in the composition of a poem. See *pattern, sensibility, worth*. Also see *fancy* and *imagination*.

tail—see BOB AND WHEEL.

TAILED SONNET—see CAUDATED SONNET.

tail-glide, 22

TANKA, 122

TANKA CHAIN, 122

TAWDDGYRCH CADWYNOG, 95–96.

telescoped metaphor—see *conceit*.

ten-line forms, 37

tenor—see *metaphoric construction*.

TERCET, 123

TERZANELLE, 125

TERZA RIMA, 124

TERZA RIMA SONNET, 124

tetrameter, 17

tetrasyllabic: comprised of four syllables.

texte, 53, 71, 101, 117

texture—see *sonics, cynghanedd*.

thirteen-line forms, 37

thirty-five-line forms, 38

thirty-line forms, 38

thirty-nine-line forms, 38

three-line forms, 33–34

THRENODY—see ELEGY.

timbre—see *sonic level*.

TODDAID, 126

tone color—see SONIC LEVEL.

TRIAD, 123

tribrach, 15

trimeter, 17

TRIOLET, 127

triple rhymes, 112, 125

TRIPLET, 128

triplet forms, 33–34

trisyllabic: comprised of three syllables.

TRIVERSEN, 130

trochee, 15

TROILUS STANZA—see RIME ROYAL.

tropes, 27–31

troubadours: medieval Provençal poets. *Jongleurs* were wandering minstrels who performed the work of the troubadours or *trouvères*, who were poets of the courts. *Minnesingers* were medieval German minstrels who both composed and performed.

true rhyme, 23

truncation—see *catalexis*.

TUMBLING VERSE—see SKELTONICS.

twelve-line forms, 37

twenty-five-line forms, 38

twenty-eight-line forms, 38

twenty-line forms, 38

two-hundred-line forms, 38

two-hundred-ten-line forms, 38

two-line forms, 33

ubi sunt motif: the "where are they?" convention of lamentation for the past.

unaccented syllable, 15, 18–19, 21–22, 59. See also *mora*.

unrhymed syllable, 19

variable accentuals—see *variable foot*.

variable foot: the accentual prosody of W.C. Williams and others. Broadly, it is a system built on three-line units: each three lines is roughly equivalent to a clause (see the TRIVERSEN). Each line is equivalent to a phrase (see breath pause). In each line there are to be found from two to four stresses, but occasionally a line will contain only one stress, or, rarely, as many as five. It is from this accentual variation within the line that the "variable" foot derives its name.

variable syllabics: the prosody of Marianne Moore and others. The lines of a single stanza of poetry may vary in length; i.e., in a five-line stanza the syllabic lengths of lines may be three, five, seven, four, and two syllables respectively. Succeeding stanzas will normally retain the same counts as the first stanza, line for line.

variable syllable: a syllable that may or may not be accented, depending on its position in the context of the poem. See also *distributed stress*.

vehicle—see *metaphoric construction*.

verbal texture—see *sonics, cynghanedd*.

vers de société: light verse concerned with manners and customs.

verse, 68, 70. See also *line of verse* and *stich*.

verse chapter—see *canto* and *fit*.

verse foot, 15

VERSE NARRATIVES, 131

verse paragraph, 69

verse sentence, 130

vers libre—see *free verse*.

Victorian poets: romantic poets of the second half of the nineteenth century.

vignette, 131

VILLANELLE, 132

VIRELAI, 77–78

virgule, 15

visible level, 21

vocalic assonance—see *assonance*.

vowels, 22–23, 44

Welsh forms, 45, 52, 57, 59, 60–62, 66–67, 73, 75, 95–96, 126, 128–129

w-glide, 22

WHEEL—see BOB AND WHEEL.

worth: a value judgment concerning the intent of a poem, and the achievement of that intent by the poet. It has been said that a poem may be worthy in one of three general ways: 1) by reason of its saying something completely new; 2) by reason of its offering a new insight or perspective on an already established idea or subject; 3) by reason of its couching an established idea or subject in a new and interesting style. See *tact, sensibility*.

wrenched accent: when, in context, the metric of the line demands that a normally unaccented syllable take a stress, the result will be wrenched accent.

wrenched rhyme, 24

word-count prosody, 70

y-glide, 22

A FRIEND IN DANGER . . .

Max received an image from Alex of pure fear, of shadowy threatening presences, of misery and loneliness. There was no place for Alex to relax or rest. He was constantly on the run. Running for his life.

What is it? Max sent out frantically. Alex, what's wrong? What are you running from?

But before Alex could reply, another being took his place—an unfriendly entity who blasted Max with images of fire and destruction. Max recoiled . . . and lost track of Alex in the whirlwind of auras.

He thrust himself into the storm, struggling to hold on to Alex's signature energy, but to no avail. The angry being had blocked Alex from further communication.

Alex, he sent, Alex, if you can hear me, we're trying to bring you back! We all miss you, and we want you to come home! I promise . . . I promise we will find a way to get you here where you belong!

Don't miss any books in this fascinating new series:

ROSWELL HIGH

#1 THE OUTSIDER
#2 THE WILD ONE
#3 THE SEEKER
#4 THE WATCHER
#5 THE INTRUDER
#6 THE STOWAWAY
#7 THE VANISHED
#8 THE REBEL
#9 THE DARK ONE
#10 THE SALVATION

Available from POCKET PULSE

ROSWELL

HIGH

THE VANISHED

by

MELINDA METZ

POCKET PULSE

New York   London   Toronto   Sydney   Singapore

POCKET PULSE, published by
Pocket Books, a division of Simon & Schuster, Inc.
1230 Avenue of the Americas, New York, NY 10020

Produced by 17th Street Productions, Inc.
33 West 17th Street
New York, NY 10011

ISBN: 0-671-03561-4

First POCKET PULSE printing May 2000

10 9 8 7 6 5 4 3 2 1

POCKET PULSE and colophon are trademarks of
Simon & Schuster Inc.

Printed in the U.S.A.

ONE

Michael Guerin caught a whiff of something fresh and tangy. The smell of the ocean. God, he loved that smell.

Yeah, but do you love it because you love the ocean? he asked himself. Or do you love it because it's the way Cameron smells?

He ignored himself. He needed to get some sleep. And thinking about Cameron Winger was like chain drinking fifty cups of coffee. It made him feel like all his nerves were vibrating.

The ocean scent grew stronger. And Michael's nerves started vibrating faster, generating an electric current that raced through his body. Cameron was here. In his room, in his bedroom. He was sure of it.

Before he could sit up, he felt her arm slip around his waist, felt her breath warm against the back of his neck. Cameron wasn't just in his bedroom. She was in his bed.

He used to fantasize about exactly this when he was lying in his cell in the Clean Slate compound, held prisoner by Sheriff Valenti. The fantasies kept him sane in there. Kept him from thinking about exactly what the Clean Slate crew planned to do with him after they learned everything they could about his powers.

But those fantasies all took place before he found out the truth about Cameron. That was before he found out that she wasn't just another prisoner in the compound. She was working for Valenti, and her job was to get Michael to give her the names of the other aliens living in Roswell.

Was he just supposed to forget that Cameron had betrayed him? Was he just supposed to what—roll over and start kissing her or something?

Yes, you big idiot! his body screamed at him. Yes! Do it. Do it now!

"Can't you even look at me?" Cameron asked softly. "You haven't actually looked at me for days."

It was true. He avoided looking at her because when he looked at her, he wanted her. And starting up something with Cameron again didn't seem like the smartest idea.

Cameron pulled her arm away. The mattress dipped as she slid to the edge of the bed.

"I guess I thought risking my life for you and your friends would mean . . ." Her words trailed off. "My mistake."

Michael shoved himself up into a sitting position and leaned against the headboard. He shot a quick glance at Cameron. She was facing away from him, and the curve of her neck under that short red hair of hers almost annihilated him. There was something about that short-as-an-army-guy hair that made the rest of her look even more female.

"It did mean something," Michael told her. "We probably wouldn't have gotten out of there alive without you."

It was true. Cameron had risked her life to help them escape from Elsevan DuPris, an enemy who had proven himself to be much more dangerous than Sheriff Valenti and Project Clean Slate. Cameron knew DuPris was an alien with powers exponentially stronger than Michael's and the others', but that hadn't stopped her from hurling herself at DuPris unarmed. Totally defenseless.

"But?" Cameron asked.

But Michael's problem was figuring out which was the real Cameron. The girl who betrayed him. Or the girl who saved his life.

He sighed. If he was going to try and explain that to her, he had to at least look her in the eye. Even if it caused some kind of electrical fire inside him.

Michael reached out and pulled Cameron around to face him. And then he screamed. He couldn't help himself.

It wasn't Cameron sitting there. Not any-more. It was DuPris.

"Wake up, Michael," DuPris told him. "You're a whole different species than that . . . girl. A superior species. Don't taint yourself."

What did DuPris want? He couldn't have taken on Cameron's appearance just to give Michael advice on his love life.

"Wake up, Michael," DuPris repeated. But it didn't sound like DuPris anymore. It sounded like Max Evans, Michael's best friend.

Michael felt a pair of hands shaking him, although DuPris hadn't touched him. DuPris wasn't even in the room anymore.

What the hell?

"I know you need your beauty sleep, but you have to wake up," Max's voice insisted.

Michael jerked upright and opened his eyes. "Thanks," he mumbled. "I was having a heinous nightmare. Cameron turned into DuPris and—" He shook his head. "You get the idea."

"Nasty," Max said. He stepped back, and Michael noticed for the first time that the rest of the group was there, too. Max's sister, Isabel, hovered by the bedroom door along with Liz Ortecho, Maria DeLuca, and Adam.

For a moment Michael wondered what he'd done to earn the honor of a group wake-up call, but then he groggily recalled the plan.

They were supposed to go out to the ruins of the Project Clean Slate compound to find their ship—the one DuPris had crashed back in 1947, killing Michael's and Max's and Isabel's parents . . . and Adam's. For years Michael had searched for the ship. Then just a few weeks ago he and his friends had discovered that Project Clean Slate, an organization dedicated to tracking down and possibly disposing of alien life on earth, had been hiding it in their secret compound for decades.

Unfortunately, Michael had only discovered the ship because Sheriff Valenti had trapped him in the compound. Michael's friends had stormed the place and broken him out, and the compound was destroyed in the process. The upside was Valenti and the rest of the Clean Slate crew were history. Ashes. Vapor. The enemy had been obliterated.

The downside was the ship might be history, too.

"So, the gang's all here," Michael said. "If I could get a little privacy, I'll get dressed and then we'll hit the road." Then he noticed the silence and the worried looks on his friends' faces. "What's up?" he asked.

Nobody replied, and a sick feeling twisted Michael's stomach. Somebody's missing, he realized, the first wings of panic fluttering in his chest. And it's not Alex. . . .

Sadly, Michael had already gotten somewhat used to the lack of Alex Manes's bright orange aura in their group. A few days had passed since Alex had been mistakenly pulled through the wormhole that Max had opened to their home planet. Max had been trying to send DuPris back there, but DuPris had tricked them all, and now DuPris was free and Alex was in a galaxy far, far, *far* away. And who knew how the beings felt about having a human tourist.

"It's Cameron," Maria said quietly, pushing a stray blond curl behind her ear.

Michael was out of bed in an instant. Without bothering to pull a pair of jeans over his boxers, he rushed into the living room and over to the pile of flattened beanbags where Cameron Winger had been crashing for the past few nights. It was vacant. Michael put his hand on the cushion closest to him and found it cold. Cameron had left hours ago.

He spun to face Adam. "Did you see her leave?"

He, Adam, and Cameron had all been staying in Ray Iburg's apartment. They figured Ray wouldn't have minded. Before he died, he'd been kind of a mentor to Michael, Max, and Isabel, the only adult survivor of the Roswell Incident crash.

At least that's what they'd all thought until Elsevan DuPris revealed the truth about himself.

"I was asleep," Adam answered, his green eyes dark with sympathy.

Max cleared his throat. "I'm sorry, man," he said, placing his hand on Michael's shoulder.

For a moment Michael was surprised to feel how weak Max's grip was. But it made sense, with all he'd been through recently.

"It's okay," Michael said, taking a deep breath. "It's fine. We have something more important to deal with right now."

He would think about Cameron later. Much

later. He wasn't going to let his feelings about some girl stop him from doing what needed to be done. Even some girl who turned him inside out, who betrayed him and saved his life.

If Max could stand up and face the disaster their lives had become, so could Michael. The withered, gray spots that had appeared on Max's face and neck after he'd opened the wormhole had faded, but he still had to be seriously exhausted. Michael was impressed that Max was even standing. His best friend was so painfully inspiring, it made Michael feel uplifted and nauseated all at the same time.

Michael grabbed a pair of pants and a T-shirt off the floor and yanked them on. "What are we waiting for?"

"To the Batmobile!" Maria cried. No one laughed. "Sorry. You know what happens when I get nervous. Brain Jell-O," she muttered.

A few minutes later all six of them were crammed into Max and Isabel's Jeep. Michael sat squashed between Adam and Max in the backseat, with Liz more or less on Max's lap. Maria was riding shotgun, and Isabel was driving.

They zoomed through the flat, strip-mall-lined streets of Roswell toward the desert beyond. The sun blared down on them, and the air over the road shimmered with haze.

"Do you think the ship will still be there?" Maria asked. Her question echoed through the silence in the Jeep like the crack of breaking ice. "I've been trying to imagine it still in the base—to visualize it. Maybe if we all do that, if we all visualize it, it will—"

"What flavor of Jell-O is that in your brain, anyway?" Isabel snapped.

Maria bit her lip and didn't say anything else.

Every muscle in Michael's body tensed. There was a *thing* between Isabel and Maria lately. And he had a feeling he was the thing. They'd both made a play for him when all he'd been thinking about was Cameron. And even though they'd both backed off, there was still this thing, this little bit of attitude. He was about to tell them to chill, but thankfully, Liz beat him to it.

"Was that necessary?" Liz asked, leaning between the two front seats and glaring at Isabel.

"Maybe," Isabel replied. Her shoulders were stiff, and she stared grimly at the road ahead of them. "I'm just not in the mood for one of Maria's little New Age games. Is that okay with you?"

"No," Liz said. "It's not."

"Everyone calm down," Max interrupted. "We're all worried. But we can't take it out on each other."

"Well, sorry if I'm paying attention to reality," Isabel said. "But did any of you stop to think that when Adam trashed the compound, it might have alerted other people? Like the police . . . or even worse, the media?"

"First of all," Michael replied, "Adam didn't blow up the Clean Slate compound. DuPris did, when he had control of Adam's body. You should understand that better than anyone, Izzy."

That was because DuPris had taken over Isabel's body, too. Just thinking about it sent a surge of bile up Michael's throat.

"I know," Isabel said. "But that doesn't change the fact that the police, or even a TV crew, could be waiting for us around the next corner."

"The explosion was a few days ago," Liz said. "The media would've been crawling all over Roswell by now if they'd heard anything." She reached back and quickly twisted her long dark hair into a spiral down her back. "I know you're freaked, but that doesn't mean you can just be randomly mean to people."

Isabel took a deep breath and let it out slowly. "I'm sorry, Maria," she said quietly. "I'm just in a mood. Don't take it personally."

"It's forgotten," Maria said.

The *thing* faded. Michael leaned forward slightly. "The ship should be undamaged," he said. "Remember that piece of metal I found out in the desert? The ship is made out of the same stuff, and nothing I did to that scrap hurt it in the least. Not even a blowtorch—"

"The ship's fine," Adam added. "I know for sure."

"Did Valenti have you test it?" Max asked.

"Yeah, we beat that thing up endlessly. Nothing I did ever hurt it at all," Adam replied, staring out the side of the Jeep.

Michael heard the distant tone of Adam's voice and felt a surge of anger. He didn't even like to imagine how Adam had been raised. The late Sheriff Valenti had imprisoned Adam in the underground compound and never let him know that there was anything outside, never taught him anything about the world. Valenti even told Adam that he was Adam's father, which to Michael pretty much defined the word *twisted*.

It made Michael's childhood shuttling between foster homes look like *The Brady Bunch*.

Maria peered over the back of her seat at Adam. "So the ship could be fine," she said. "It could have survived DuPris nuking the place. All we have to do is dig it up, hop in, and zip off to get Alex and bring him back."

Michael glanced at Max, and the concerned, caged look in his best friend's eyes told him Max was thinking the same thing he was—if only it were that easy.

"Even if the ship's okay, we've still got to figure out how to fly it," Michael said. "Then if we manage that—"

"We still don't know how to get there," Max broke in. "I mean, I could get general instructions and directions by linking to the collective consciousness, but there's a big difference between being told how to do something and actually *doing* it. None of us has a clue about space travel. What if the flight takes years?"

Maria's eyes were wide. "Yeah, but it's *possible,* right?"

"We wouldn't be coming back out here if it wasn't," Isabel replied.

It's possible, Michael thought. It just isn't very likely.

But he wasn't about to squash Maria's hopes—and the hopes of everyone in the Jeep—by saying that out loud.

Hope was all they had left.

"We've arrived," Isabel said, slowing the Jeep to a crawl. She pulled up alongside a massive stretch of ground that was so burned, it gleamed like onyx, the rocks in the soil fused into a glassy sheen by the blast of Adam's energy. Make that Adam's energy combined with and controlled by DuPris's.

The six of them clambered out. "It's under there," Adam said. He pointed to a section near the center, staring at the ground as if he could see through it. "Deep."

Max led the way, kicking at the scorched sand. "Looks like we're in for some serious digging."

"We didn't bring shovels," Maria said, raising her hand over her eyes to shield them from the sun.

"We've got us," Isabel replied, locking eyes with Michael.

Maria blushed. "Oh, right. The not-quite-human bulldozers."

"I'm still weak," Max said. "I don't know how much use I'll be—"

"The four of us can connect," Michael interrupted him. "We'll get it done faster that way."

Liz turned to Maria. "Come on," she said. "Let's go keep watch."

"Ma'am, yes ma'am!" Maria said with a little salute. "Always wanted to do that," she said, grinning.

Michael smiled. Even in a situation as tense as this one, Maria always managed to do something that lightened his mood.

Isabel, Adam, Max, and Michael linked hands, forming a circle, and the connection was instantaneous. The four of them were one. Michael felt their auras flood through him, mingling with his own brick red energy. Isabel's rich purple blended with Max's emerald green, and then Adam's yellow aura shot through the mixture like a powerful blast of pure sunlight. Together they composed their combined force into a sturdy dark brown reservoir of power. Their individual scents—Michael's eucalyptus, Max's cedar, Isabel's cinnamon, and Adam's innocent smell of green leaves—intermingled to create a no-nonsense odor of burning wood. They focused their energy toward the molecules of the scorched dirt in front of them.

Michael felt power leap from them as they began to unravel the fused atoms of the blasted ground. It was tough going. The energy of Adam's earlier attack had sealed the soil into a dense blacktop, and that material was extremely difficult to break apart.

Then Adam released an image into their combined selves. It showed the group sharpening their energy to slice *between* the molecules rather than pulling them apart like a loaf of bread. Michael had never tried that before, but since Adam knew how, now Michael knew how. In a moment they had managed to cut open the crust and peel it back in a long strip.

Underneath, the dirt was crumbly and dry and much easier to move. They pushed it up the sides of the opening they'd made so that the soil gathered like an anthill.

Max was starting to leak images of his bedroom along with a general sense of weariness. He wouldn't be able to keep this up much longer. Michael sent him a strong boost of energy, diverting some of his force from the task at hand.

Foot by foot, the wide cone of dirt grew around the deepening hole. Chunks of wood and cement came flying up along with the dust of plaster as they tunneled through the crushed roof of the hangar. Never breaking the connection, they all walked forward until they were standing on the lip of the hole, peering downward at the churning vortex. And then Michael saw it—they all saw it—the smooth, dark metallic gray crescent of the ship's hull. The unearthly metal gleamed and rippled in the sunlight as if it were alive.

Keep going, Michael urged Isabel, Max, and Adam. We're almost there. He tried to calm his excitement, which would only break his concentration.

"A car!" Liz called.

"Someone's coming!" Maria shouted.

Michael dropped Isabel's and Adam's hands and wheeled around to look. In the distance a plume of dust was rising over the dirt road, heading their way.

"Back to the Jeep!" Isabel cried. "Now!" She rushed up and over the hill of debris they'd made, and Adam, Max, and Michael scrambled behind her. When he reached the top, Michael spun back and gave the hill a mental shove, which started a small avalanche. He wasn't sure if it would cover the ship, but it was all he had time to do.

Michael turned and ran up to the driver's side door, where he saw that Isabel had already started the Jeep. "I'm driving," he told her.

"There's no way." Isabel fixed him with a look of panic and fierce determination in her blue eyes.

"You're right," Michael said. "You'll be faster." He climbed into the backseat beside Adam.

Maria let out a short scream as the Jeep lurched and screeched over the charred earth around them. Isabel took a sharp turn toward the open desert, and Michael twisted around in his seat to look out the back. In the bright sunlight he couldn't get a good look at the approaching car, but it was close enough to have seen them, and it looked like it was speeding up.

"It's chasing us," Liz reported. "Go faster, Isabel."

"I'm trying!" Isabel called.

"Blow out its tires!" Maria shouted. "Adam, can't you blow out its tires?"

"We're moving too fast for me to aim," Adam answered.

There was no way they could slow down. The car was gaining on them. Michael didn't care who the people in it were. They could be military, police, Clean Slate, reporters—nobody could discover the truth about Michael and his friends. He had to figure a way to protect them—his friends—his family.

"We need cover," Michael said, peering around at the loosely vegetated ground up ahead. Cacti and sagebrush grew in clumps all over the desert floor, and the Jeep was bouncing over them as Isabel sped along. Nothing Michael could see was tall enough to help them hide.

"Behind what?" Isabel argued. "There's nothing around for miles."

"There's got to be a ravine or something," Max said. "Someplace where we can lose them."

"They can see us," Liz said. "How are we going to get far enough ahead of them to lose them anywhere?"

For a second everybody in the Jeep was silent, thinking, as the desert whizzed by outside.

"Got it," Liz said. "Use your powers to whip up a dust storm or something. It'll give us some headway, and it won't even look weird. Dust storms happen out here all the time."

Max gave Liz a quick kiss on the lips. "I knew we kept you around for a reason," he joked. "Do you think we can do it?"

Michael shrugged. "We were just digging. Why not?"

"All right," Max said. "We're going to need all of us for this. Except you, Iz. You keep a lookout for anywhere we can hide for a while."

"Got it," Isabel said.

Michael reached out and took Maria's and Adam's hands while everyone else linked up. Liz and Maria couldn't focus their energy on their own, but adding their amber and sapphire essences to the mix strengthened the group overall. Together they spun the elements of the ground along their trail into motion, whipping the reddish dirt into the air until it clouded behind them in a haze.

It's working! Liz sent the message out to the others. I can't believe it's working.

More, Max urged them. Thicker, darker, *more*.

Luckily Isabel had located a low path into a wide canyon where the ground was covered with the eroded sand of the rock walls. The fine silt was easy to whirl into the storm they'd created. Michael could no longer see the car chasing them, which meant the mystery driver couldn't see them, either.

Isabel cut a hairpin turn down the flat slope of a

dry riverbed off the canyon. The arroyo wound around an outcropping of sculpted tan rock before splitting into two branches.

Isabel careened the Jeep down the branch to the left, and after a hundred yards or so of wild driving, she brought the Jeep up short behind a grove of stubby trees growing at a bend in the arroyo. With the added cover their pursuers just might miss them entirely.

"Keep it up," Isabel said. "I think we lost them, but I don't want to take any chances." She connected into the group through Maria, adding her anxious energy to the mix.

Michael continued to concentrate on keeping the dirt molecules in motion, but it was draining. Other questions kept intruding, questions he shared with his friends through their link.

Who was that chasing us? Obviously whoever was in the other car didn't just stumble on the compound, or they wouldn't have raced to follow them.

So who was it?

And what exactly did they want?

Time to call home, Max thought. After cleaning the dusty day off his body in the shower, Max lay in bed, propped up by pillows. He was ready to go to sleep, but first he wanted to make a connection to the collective consciousness.

Max hadn't linked in since he'd combined

power with the consciousness to open the wormhole. Building that passage had exhausted him nearly to the point of death, and tonight was the first time he'd felt strong enough to even make an attempt at connecting.

In truth, it had been a relief to take a break from visiting the collective consciousness over the past few days. The billions of voices demanding information from him could be overpowering.

But he thought he felt up to connecting tonight.

Max closed his eyes. Breathed in a shaky but deep breath. Let himself relax.

Let himself reach out.

Let himself open up.

The ocean of auras that made up the consciousness was waiting for him, expecting him. Max plunged into the chaos of intertwined beings and was inundated by questioning images.

There was a new ripple of disturbance in the collective perceptions, a shock wave of bright orange confusion. Alex. Confusion over Alex. Confusion and anger and fear and excitement.

Max felt a burst of relief. Alex was alive. He'd made it alive to the home planet. Max had never shared his doubts with his friends, but he'd never been sure if a human could survive the trip through space.

His awful mistake—sending Alex instead of DuPris through the wormhole—no longer lay like a heavy, wet blanket across his shoulders. Alex was alive!

But Max's relief was short-lived. Intense images bubbled up from a pocket of the consciousness depicting Alex as a frightening foreigner, his friendly features exaggerated, a portrait painted by fear and distrust of the unknown.

Alex is my friend, Max shared with the collective, hoping to explain—to calm their fears. *He was sent to you by accident. My accident.*

A ruffle of interest spiked with doubt and animosity greeted his thoughts, and Max realized he had to talk to them in their own way, recall the sights and sounds and smells of that day and surrender the memory to the consciousness.

Max started with an image of himself struggling to open the wormhole—an event many in the consciousness remembered vividly. They returned their own recollections of painful effort and exhaustion.

Then Max sent a picture of his friends morphing their faces and bodies to look like DuPris in a desperate attempt to buy Max the time he needed. The consciousness reacted with fury to the image of the traitor. DuPris had stolen one of the Stones of Midnight from the planet, and they hated him for robbing them of the sacred power source.

When Max showed DuPris tricking the group into forcing Alex through the wormhole, the collective's fury was whipped into rage. Their anger was so potent that Max wondered if he should disconnect before the strength of their emotion did him damage.

But he had to stay strong. Max focused on channeling their wrath away from Alex. Too many of the voices in the collective were associating him with their feelings about DuPris, and that could be deadly. Max had to let them know what Alex was really like.

He started off with the strongest image of Alex he could remember—Alex sitting in front of Isabel's closed bedroom door, keeping a vigil when Isabel was too destroyed over the death of her boyfriend Nikolas to get out of bed. Alex had stayed there, talking to Isabel through the door, saying anything that popped into his mind—jokes, stories, one-sided arguments—anything to keep Isabel connected to the world. His patience had been endless, and his inventive mind had never run out of things to say.

A murmur rolled through the network of beings. A good number of them turned their attention to Max, and he could feel them considering his image of Alex as a good friend.

What else could he tell them to make them understand?

Humor, Max thought. Above all else, Alex is funny.

Would the web of alien minds understand human humor? Max had to try—any picture of Alex would be incomplete unless his humor was factored in. He concentrated on sharing memories of Alex at his goofiest.

Alex mocking DuPris with an overdone, corn-fried southern accent.

Alex making his silly lists to post on the Internet. The twenty best-tasting fried snack foods. The ugliest American presidents in order of hideousness, from Taft to Kennedy. The top ten reasons why goldfish made lousy pets. The fifty funniest words in the English language. (Number one was *panty*.)

Even when Alex was most down, when he was crushed over Isabel or struggling against his got-to-be-a-military-man father, that spark of light that allowed him to find the humor in any situation never went out.

Max tried to express this all to the consciousness, flashing memories of Alex goofing around, his friends cracking up beside him. The collective absorbed those memories, and Max was relieved to feel amusement from some of the beings in response.

They were getting what Max was trying to tell them.

That Alex was good, Alex was his friend. It was as easy and as difficult to express as that.

There were still some rumblings in the corners of the collective that insisted Alex didn't belong on their planet. Dark rumblings.

Max couldn't agree more. He wanted Alex back on earth more than any of them. Max sent an image of the beings in the consciousness forming another wormhole and sending Alex back. Could they do it?

No, came the reply, they couldn't. Max received a sense of pure weariness and exhaustion from the friendlier members of the collective. A picture of a group of glowing moons traveling slowly through a dark, acid green sky flashed in front of him. Because he didn't know how fast the moons passed over the home planet, Max couldn't be sure how long it would take before the beings in the consciousness were recovered enough to send Alex back. But he understood that it would be a long while.

Max suddenly felt very tired. He wasn't strong enough for this kind of prolonged communication yet.

But before he detached himself, he sent one last message into the darkness.

Tell Alex I'm going to help him. Please tell him I'll find a way to bring him back.

He wasn't sure if the message would get to his friend, but it was the best he could do. Max separated from the collective consciousness and let himself slump down in his soft bed. Every limb on his body felt like it weighed about a hundred pounds.

All he could do now was wait. Wait and hope the collective would get his message to Alex. Hope that he could figure out a way to get his friend home.

TWO

Isabel couldn't relax. All her usual tricks—organizing her jewelry, refolding all her clothes, giving her long blond hair one hundred strokes with a brush—had failed her tonight. She had even arranged the shoes in her closet by designer, subdivided by color, but that hadn't calmed her down, either. Isabel stood in the center of her room, surveying the impeccable order. There was nothing left that needed to be done.

Flopping down on her back on the fluffy bed, Isabel let out a long sigh. As soon as she closed her eyes, she thought about Alex. Alex, who she was trying so hard to avoid thinking about. Alex, who had loved her far more than she had deserved.

She missed him. That sounded so lame. Like he was on vacation with his parents or something. But she couldn't think of a better way to say it. She missed him.

Isabel turned onto her side, pulling her legs up to her chest. Things had been bad between them before he disappeared. And it was her fault. Guilt—her least favorite emotion—churned in her gut.

She sat up on the edge of the bed, clutching a

pillow to her chest. You apologized to him for the way you broke up with him, she reminded herself.

Not that some lame apology could make up for the way she'd done the deed. She'd been ruthless and harsh. Maybe there wasn't any good way to break up with somebody, but *any* other way would have been better than the irrational tirade she'd subjected him to.

A memory of how hurt Alex's eyes had looked when she'd told him off forced its way into Isabel's mind. He had loved her, through some intensely bad times. He'd always been there, even when she tried to shove him away. And how had she repaid him?

Isabel covered her eyes with her hands.

She'd treated him like a toilet.

Flush.

Isabel couldn't stand it any longer. She had to do something to make herself feel better. She hopped to her feet and shook out her arms. Maybe she should exercise a little—sweat it out of her system. Or she could reorganize her nail polish, maybe catch up on some homework. She glanced at her small white desk.

Or she could write a letter to Alex.

Before she could convince herself that writing a letter to someone trapped in another galaxy was a waste of time, Isabel sat down and pulled out a piece of cream-colored stationery. She grabbed a green fountain pen and started to write.

Dear Alex,

Now what? Should she say she'd be waiting for him when he came back, in that girlfriend kind of way? She nibbled on the end of her pen cap. Even if Alex still wanted that, she wasn't sure if she did. She decided to stick with what she knew with absolute certainty.

> *I need you to know how much I care about you. You've been a true friend to me. I miss you every day you're gone. I miss the way you acted like the entire world was created just for me. You're the sweetest guy I've ever met, and I know we need to be important to each other, in whatever way that turns out to be.*
> *I hope you're safe. And believe me when I say that I will do anything in my power to make sure you get back to us safely. Soon.*
> *Love,*
> *Isabel*

Isabel put the pen down on the desk and stared at the long letter in front of her. God, it was so mushy—so unlike her. But she couldn't deny that she'd been as honest in it as she knew how to be. She wished she could give it to Alex. If he could read it, Isabel was certain he'd forgive her.

But Alex was trapped in another galaxy. That would take some serious postage.

In a flash, she had an idea. It was a goofy plan, but that meant Alex would love it. Isabel grabbed the paper and folded it into her pocket.

Twenty minutes later she was driving the Jeep through the desert. The night was chilly, and Isabel pulled her pink-and-gray sweater close to her skin.

A mile or so away from the site Isabel pulled over to the side of the road. Before she got out of the Jeep, she opened the glove compartment and took out the bottle rocket she'd brought with her. Her father loved the Fourth of July, and he always kept extra fireworks in a metal box in the garage. The box had been locked, but a simple turnkey clasp couldn't keep out someone with Isabel's powers.

Isabel tied the rolled-up letter to the bottle rocket, high enough on the thin red stick so that the paper wouldn't get burned. Then she got out of the Jeep and walked a few paces into the scrubby vegetation of the desert.

Isabel stuck the bottle rocket into the ground, leaning it against a small rock. Then she realized she'd forgotten to bring matches.

Not a problem. She took a deep breath, reached out with her mind toward the wick, and *scratched*. The friction produced a tiny spark, which was enough to get the wick sizzling.

As she stepped back, the rocket launched, whistling into the dark sky. Isabel watched its smoky path through the air until she lost sight of it against the canopy of stars.

Go, she thought. Go to Alex. Tell him how I feel.

The only reply was a sharp report and a shower of sparks as the rocket exploded in the distance.

Isabel smiled as she looked out across the desert. She'd just done a really silly thing, but it made her feel slightly better, and that was all that mattered.

A sudden breeze picked up, and Isabel realized with a chill that she wasn't far from the ruins of the compound. An inexplicable fist of fear gripped her heart, erasing any warm and fuzzy Alex feelings. She felt like she was being watched.

Okay. Enough with the midnight hike, Isabel thought.

She turned and hurried back to the Jeep, fully prepared to gun the engine and speed back to town. But the moment she slammed the door behind her, she realized she was acting like a child. No one was watching her. There was nothing out here for miles. She was perfectly safe.

And just to prove it to herself, she was going to drive over to the charred stretch of ground and check on the ship. It was the least she could do since she was already out here.

As she drove through the eerie darkness of the desert, Isabel felt the uneasiness start to creep up her spine again, and she gripped the steering wheel tightly. She tried to ignore the fear, but she couldn't. All she could do was defy it.

Something told her to stop a quarter mile from the compound and walk the rest of the way. Anyone who might be watching would see the headlights—hear the engine. But Isabel wouldn't give in. Swallowing back her instincts, she floored the accelerator and drove right up to the perimeter of the compound.

Taking a deep breath, Isabel stepped out of the Jeep and looked around defiantly, tossing her long blond hair over her shoulder.

See? There's no one here, she told herself, climbing the small hill she, Max, Michael, and Adam had formed while digging the hole.

"Valenti's dead, so no Valenti," she muttered, scrambling over the loose dirt. "No DuPris. No cops. No news anchors—"

Isabel reached the top of the hill and looked down into the gaping hole. Her heart dropped through her hiking shoes, and she sucked in a sharp breath.

"No . . . ship," she said quietly.

She *shoved* at the dirt with her mind. The digging went much slower now that she was alone, but she went deep enough to convince herself that she was right.

The hole was empty.

The ship was gone.

* * *

28

"The ship doesn't look anything like that," Adam said, stopping in the middle of Main Street. He pointed at a big plastic flying saucer that had been built into the side of a tourist souvenir shop as if it had crashed there.

Michael slammed into him from behind and gave him a little shove to get him moving again. A car sped by, narrowly missing their heels.

"Okay, you can't be stopping in the middle of the street like that," Michael said, trying hard to keep his voice from sounding harsh. "We'll be dead before we ever get to breakfast."

Adam wandered over to the souvenir store, staring up at the pseudo–flying saucer.

"Too bad it's not the real one," Michael said, standing next to Adam. "But somehow I don't think whoever stole it is going to make it that easy to find."

"Whoever?" Adam asked, raising his eyebrows. "I just figured that Project Clean Slate had it."

Michael's stomach twisted just from hearing the organization's name. "Clean Slate's history, remember? The place was flattened." He eyed Adam carefully. "Unless . . . wait," Michael said. "You don't know of other compounds or something, do you? There aren't . . . more of them."

Adam shrugged. "Not that I know of, I guess."

Michael wished he'd sounded a little more definite. Swallowing hard, Michael stared up at the fake ship. If there were more Clean Slate agents out there and if they'd somehow gotten the ship . . .

"How will we get Alex back now?" Adam asked, putting Michael's fears into words.

Michael's stomach turned. "I don't know," he replied. "We'll think of something."

"Can we get some toast for breakfast?" Adam asked suddenly.

"No toast," Michael said, managing a small smile. Adam's life was so simple. But Michael supposed that was what happened when you grew up with no knowledge of the outside world. "This morning I've got a surprise for you."

Michael led Adam down the sidewalk toward the doughnut shop on the corner. Wait till Adam gets his first taste of crullers with hot sauce, Michael thought. I'll never hear about toast again— it'll be doughnut shop, doughnut shop, doughnut shop until we feed him his first slice of enchilada with toothpaste.

As soon as Michael opened the door of the tiny shop, he was hit by a blast of greasy, sweet-smelling heat. He looked up at the rack behind the counter to see which doughnuts were left and caught a glimpse of mustard-colored aura out of the corner of his eye. A very familiar aura.

Two places ahead in line was Mr. Cuddihy, Michael's social worker.

Damn, Michael thought. He hadn't been home to his foster family, the Pascals, in a week or so.

Hadn't been to school, either. First he was in the compound. Then he was trying to save their collective butts from DuPris. And now there was the Alex situation. There was no way he could follow all the Pascals' two billion rules and do what needed to be done to get Alex home.

He had to get out of there, pronto. He grabbed Adam and started to steer him toward the door.

"Michael, wait, what's a bagel?" Adam asked in a loud voice. "Can I get it toasted? With butter?"

At the sound of Michael's name, Mr. Cuddihy turned around and locked eyes with him.

Michael froze in his tracks. Busted. He gave his social worker a shrug and a rueful smile.

Mr. Cuddihy stepped out of line and put his arm around Michael's shoulders. "Look who it is!" he said. "Michael Guerin, my favorite magician. I heard you've pulled off quite a disappearing act."

Cuddihy's idea of humor. Ha. Ha.

"You heard that, huh?" Michael said. "Listen, I can explain—"

"No need," Cuddihy interrupted. "I don't know what you had planned this morning, Guerin, but your plans have changed. You and I have an immediate appointment back at my office."

"I'll meet up with you later," Michael told Adam. He definitely didn't want Cuddihy asking the toast boy any questions.

"Much later," Cuddihy added.

Great, Michael thought. I wish my powers included the ability to mute people.

Michael faced Mr. Cuddihy across a large cluttered desk. Mr. Cuddihy's office was cramped and reeked of the peppermints he ate constantly since he quit smoking, but Michael had spent so many hours in this room that he felt comfortable. Comfortable enough to space out during Cuddihy's predictably endless lecture on responsibility.

After a few minutes Cuddihy seemed to be winding down, more or less, so Michael tuned him in again.

". . . without even calling," Cuddihy was saying. "That doesn't sound like any kind of respect to me. The Pascals were good enough to take you into their home, give you a roof over your head, and you didn't even let them know if you were dead or alive. And it was something that could have been avoided if you'd bothered to pick up the phone."

"When you're right, you're right," Michael said.

"Well, you're going to call them and apologize," Mr. Cuddihy said. "In fact, I want to hear from them that you did some serious groveling."

"No problem," Michael replied.

For a moment Mr. Cuddihy gazed at Michael in silence. Finally he let out a long sigh. "The Pascals and I weren't the only people looking for you, you know."

That got Michael's attention. He sat up straight

in the metal folding chair, causing a loud, obnoxious creak. All the tiny hairs on his neck stood on end.

"Who?" he blurted out. Had the Clean Slate people tracked him down? Had DuPris contacted his social worker? "Who else?"

"Oh, I doubt you know these people," Mr. Cuddihy said. "They had some news to share with you . . . good news, actually."

"Who?" Michael repeated.

"A legal firm representing a man named Ray Iburg," Mr. Cuddihy answered. "I believe you knew him, although I'm not sure how."

Ray? Michael thought. What could Ray's lawyers possibly want with him? He wasn't even aware that Ray *had* lawyers.

"My friend Max worked for him at the UFO museum," Michael explained slowly. "We both hung out there a lot. He gave us our own sets of keys."

Mr. Cuddihy nodded. "That's not all he's given you," he said. "Iburg's lawyers have informed me that there was a very interesting clause in his will, which he added recently."

"Yeah?" Michael said, clueless as to where this was going.

"Oh yes," Mr. Cuddihy said. "The upshot of the clause is that if Iburg didn't check in with his lawyers for one month, they were to take immediate action. All of Mr. Iburg's belongings—including the museum, the apartment, the car, and everything contained therein—are to be turned over to you, Mr. Michael Guerin, free and clear, for use as you see fit."

Michael stared at Mr. Cuddihy. He couldn't believe what he was hearing.

"I told you it was good news," said Mr. Cuddihy. "See, this is why I'm someone you should keep in touch with."

"There has to be a catch," Michael said. This wasn't the kind of thing that happened to him.

"No catch," Mr. Cuddihy said. "It's a bizarre request, but it's legal. And since good things seem to be heading your way at this point in time, I thought I'd help out a little myself. There's no reason to torture the Pascals with your presence any longer."

Michael blinked at his social worker. "What are you saying?" he asked.

Mr. Cuddihy smiled. "I've decided to help you get emancipated minor status. You're almost eighteen, anyway, and now that you have your own place to stay and you have the museum for income, I figured we could ease social services' burden of taking care of you. I don't see any reason why you shouldn't live on your own."

Michael sat back in his chair and gaped at Cuddihy. "Really?" he choked out.

"Really," Mr. Cuddihy confirmed. "Of course, you'd still have to stay in contact with me until your birthday, but our biweekly meetings should be more than sufficient." He popped another peppermint, chomped it. "Michael, I know you've had a rough time over the years, and you've handled shuffling between homes better than anyone had a right to expect. It's my pleasure to tell you congratulations. And good luck. So how does this all sound to you?"

"It sounds . . . it sounds unbelievable," Michael said. He pushed himself out of his chair as Mr. Cuddihy came out from behind the desk. Michael reached out his hand for a handshake.

"Enough with the formality," Mr. Cuddihy said. "I'm happy for you, Michael." Before Michael had time to back away, Mr. Cuddihy reached out and gave him a bear hug. Michael stiffened automatically, but as he looked down at the social worker who had kept an eye out for him for years and who now had set him free—*free*—Michael couldn't help patting the guy on the back.

"Thank you," Michael said as Mr. Cuddihy let go.

"You have to promise me you'll show up for our meetings," Mr. Cuddihy said, trying to be businesslike again. "That's a firm condition of this whole deal."

Michael stood beside the social worker, what felt like a totally dorky grin on his face. A meeting every other week? For no more foster home boogie? For being able to live on his own? For being in control of his own life?

"I'll be there," Michael promised. "You can count on me."

THREE

Liz wandered down the aisle of the auditorium at school, searching the rows for a glimpse of Max's shaggy blond hair. The auditorium was packed with students—all there for a mysterious all-school assembly during the period before lunch.

Finally she spotted Max a few seats in from the aisle in the middle of the auditorium. She squeezed through the row and plopped down into the empty seat beside him.

"Hey," she said. "Any idea what this is all about?"

"Huh?" Max replied. He turned to face her, and his beautiful silvery blue eyes seemed glazed.

"The assembly," Liz said. "Do you know what it's about?"

"Oh . . . no," Max said. He offered her a weak smile. "Sorry, I was . . . I was thinking about something else."

"Alex?" Liz asked.

Max nodded. "The ship was the only hope we had of getting him back. I mean, it was a long shot, but it was a shot."

Liz reached up and brushed a lock of hair out of

his weary eyes. "All of us are going to have to get together later and figure out what to do," she said.

"Yeah," Max said, leaning back and closing his eyes. "I'm drawing a blank."

Liz peered at his gaunt, drawn face. He looked a little stronger than he had yesterday but was still obviously worn-out. He was gorgeous, of course, but Liz was starting to think that Max would look gorgeous to her if his hair fell out and he erupted in oozing volcanic zits. She was that far gone.

"You okay?" she asked.

Max turned to face the stage as the principal, Ms. Shaffer, walked toward the podium.

"I'll live," Max said. His voice sounded far away, as if it was an effort to speak.

Slumping back into the hard wooden seat, Liz thought that maybe he should have taken a sick day and spent the day with Rosie and Jerry and Ricki. She knew he couldn't tell his parents the real reason he was feeling so out of it, but couldn't he have pretended he had the flu or something so he could get some rest?

She was about to ask him that very question when Ms. Shaffer called for attention. The auditorium got a fraction quieter as the lights dimmed. Liz waited for Max to take her hand, but he continued to stare straight ahead, his hands clasped together in his lap. Wasn't this the guy who said touching her was absolutely essential, like breathing?

Well, it's not like he doesn't have a lot on his mind, Liz thought, swallowing her disappointment. She knew that Max felt responsible for everything that happened to anyone in their group of friends, and that meant he had to be blaming himself for what had happened to Alex. Which was an *accident*. Or more accurately, it was DuPris's fault. Certainly not Max's fault.

As Ms. Shaffer blathered on about someone she was very pleased to introduce to them all, Liz leaned against Max's shoulder and concentrated on sending him happy, positive love energy. Maria would approve.

Liz decided that she would find a way to distract Max once the assembly was over. She basked in his nearness, wishing they could be alone together right now. The moment they had some privacy, she'd give him the kind of kiss that was guaranteed to take his mind off his problems, at least for a little while.

"Okay, everyone," Ms. Shaffer called, "may I present Kasey Dodson, the new interim sheriff of Roswell!"

Liz sat up, suddenly alert, and exchanged a startled look with Max as the crowd of students around her applauded halfheartedly. She shouldn't have been surprised—after all, Sheriff Valenti had been killed at the Clean Slate compound. Even though no one but them knew that's what had happened, everyone knew the sheriff was gone. Obviously the town would have to appoint someone new. But

Sheriff Valenti had been such a mainstay of her nightmares that Liz hadn't even allowed herself to consider that he might be replaced.

But here she was, the new sheriff. Liz watched as Sheriff Dodson walked toward the podium. She was a tough-looking woman with shoulder-length dark hair and a lean, muscular body under her brown uniform.

"Thank you, Principal Shaffer," Sheriff Dodson said with a smile. She had a warm, smoky voice that made her sound friendly, but Liz wasn't going to be fooled by that. She knew better than to be taken in by appearances—after all, Liz was dating an alien disguised as a human.

"Roswell has never been a town with a high crime rate, and I pledge to do my best to keep it that way," Sheriff Dodson continued. "This town has always been safe to enjoy even at night . . . and barring an alien attack, I see no reason why that shouldn't continue to be true."

Most of the students laughed at her joke. Everyone in Roswell loved its weird reputation as UFO central. But a shudder ran through Liz from head to toe.

What did she mean by that? Liz wondered, rubbing her arms to ward off the sudden chill that had invaded her body. Was she joking, or was that a threat? Is she another Clean Slate agent like Valenti?

Liz glanced at Max. He was shaking his head. He had to be as worried about this new development—if not more.

She crossed her arms over her chest, trying to calm her pounding heart.

Liz and her friends would have to watch Sheriff Dodson carefully . . . very carefully. Valenti had come uncomfortably close to discovering Max, Isabel, and Michael's secret. In fact, he *had* discovered it. He'd just been killed before he could tell anyone.

Liz knew that Michael thought Project Clean Slate was destroyed along with the compound, but Liz wasn't so sure. It was quite possible that the organization existed outside of Roswell. And if it did, it made sense that Project Clean Slate would place another of their group in a hot spot like Roswell.

Just what we need, Liz thought. Something new to worry about.

Four months ago her biggest worries had been getting to work on time, making valedictorian, and making sure her parents never had to worry that she'd end up like her sister, Rosa, dead from an overdose. She'd been constantly stressed, but that was nothing compared to obsessing over whether or not some secret agency—or some evil alien—was going to show up one day and kill you and your friends. Or that one of your friends might never make it back from another planet. It was insane. If only she could make everything go back to normal so she could hang out with Maria and Alex, make out with Max, study for SATs, and just worry about stuff like the prom—

Stop. You've got to deal with reality before it deals with you, Liz told herself. No matter how twisted reality is.

". . . and if you need to talk about anything or if you have something to report, please don't hesitate to stop by the station," Sheriff Dodson said. "I'm looking forward to getting to know all of you very well."

The students applauded, but the sheriff's words sent a shiver racing down Liz's spine.

I'm looking forward to getting to know all of you very well.

Liz had to make sure that never happened.

Max was in shock.

As he filed out of the auditorium beside Liz, so many worries demanded attention in his mind that he couldn't keep track of them all. How to get Alex back. How to find the ship. How to find DuPris and deal with him. How to keep connecting to the collective consciousness without risking permanent brain damage. How to keep his alien identity secret. And how to avoid a new sheriff who might or might not be someone who wanted him dead.

Max followed Liz through the dispersing crowd in the hall. How was he supposed to handle all this stress while feeling more exhausted than he'd ever been? He was so turned around and tired that he felt like his whole life was happening underwater. And he knew he needed to be alert in order to survive.

"Hey, Max, are you there?" Liz asked.

He looked up to find that he'd followed her up the stairs and over to the supply room across from the bio lab.

"Wait. Shouldn't we be in the cafeteria?" Max asked.

Liz opened the supply-room door and stepped in. "Get in here," she said with a mischievous smile.

Max hesitated. "I don't think we're allowed—"

Liz groaned, grabbed his arm, and yanked him into the room with her, closing the door behind him.

Max leaned against a wall next to shelves covered with battered microscopes and Bunsen burners. "So what did you think of Kasey Dodson?" he asked. "Think I have another psycho stalker?"

"Besides me?" she asked. She used her body to press him up against the wall. "I don't know about you, but the smell of formaldehyde . . . it makes me crazy."

Max just looked at her, his brain a cluttered fog. "Crazy?"

Liz put her hands on his shoulders and kissed him on the lips. Instantly the fog started to clear.

"Oh," Max said when she pulled away. "Crazy." He smiled as he tucked his hands under the hair that fell like a thick, silky curtain around her face.

He pulled her closer, releasing a long exhalation of breath as her warm, soft body pressed against his. How could he have allowed his worries to interfere with getting his minimum daily requirement of Liz? He was so stressed, he hadn't even been thinking about kissing her, and that was wrong. Deeply wrong.

His lips found hers again, and he opened himself up to the intense passion of their kiss. Liz tasted sweet and deliciously alive. Max could feel his heart racing as her tongue glided across his own, sending tingles of pleasure echoing throughout his body. As always, kissing Liz made him feel inside out, as if all of himself was concentrated on the one small, soft spot where they were connected. It was the best feeling Max could ever imagine.

As he lost himself in her, a strange sensation started to creep up his neck, tingling over his scalp. Suddenly his mind seemed to open, as if it were exposed to the universe. And then the myriad beings of the consciousness made themselves known, reacting to his and Liz's kiss. Confusion, curiosity, pleasure, amusement—Max received all of those emotions in flickering images. They wanted to know what Max was doing, and they were there to share it with him.

Startled by the unexpected intrusion, Max pulled away from Liz abruptly. He hadn't even tried to connect to the consciousness.

Liz's beautiful brown eyes fluttered open in confusion. "What?" Liz asked, sounding hurt. "What's the matter? Did I bite you or something?"

"No, no," Max assured her. "I just felt a little . . .

dizzy for a second, that's all." And violated, he added silently.

Liz searched his eyes. "Are you okay?"

"I'm fine," Max said, attempting to smile. He couldn't tell Liz what had happened. She was already distrustful of the collective because of the physical effects connecting had on Max. If he told her about the intrusion, she'd be even more freaked out than he was. "It was nothing. Maybe all that formaldehyde went to my head." He smiled at her. "Or maybe it was you."

This time, as he leaned forward to kiss her, Max focused part of his attention on blocking the consciousness from trespassing again. He managed to keep them away, but it took effort—effort he should have been focusing on Liz. And he couldn't shake the creepy feeling that he was no longer completely alone with her.

"Is everybody coming over now?" Adam asked Michael.

"In a little while," Michael replied. He picked up a tiny plastic rocket ship off the floor of the museum and placed it on a shelf. "We're going to try to figure out what to do now that the ship's been stolen and maybe do a little work on this place at the same time."

Adam's eyes swept over the museum. He didn't remember trashing the place, but he had when DuPris had turned him into the Adam puppet.

"Is Liz coming?" Adam asked, trying to sound casual. He picked up another rocket and set it next to Michael's.

"Yeah. She and Maria and Isabel and Max," Michael answered as he continued to reorganize the shelves.

Adam smiled. He did that every time someone said the name Liz. They didn't even have to be talking about his Liz. Well, Max's Liz, really. Liz Ortecho. They could be talking about any Liz, and Adam's lips would just start to curve up. Sometimes just the sound of the letter *l* was enough to do it.

"Let's turn on some music," Michael suggested, walking over to a big, mailbox-shaped machine in the corner. The machine had lots of blinking lights in it, along with rows of strange silver disks.

"What is that thing?" Adam asked, gathering up the pieces of a broken table.

"This is a jukebox," Michael explained. "Have you ever heard Elvis? Ray was definitely an Elvis man."

"What's Elvis?" Adam asked. He hated asking questions like that. It made him feel like such a baby. But that's what *Dad* Valenti had wanted. A baby who depended on his daddy for everything—including information. He'd never even given Adam anything to read besides picture books.

Adam had been logging in some major hours on Max's laptop since he escaped from the compound, but there were still way too many things he was clueless about.

Michael laughed. "Not what, *who*. Elvis was a guy. He was the king of rock. Man! You've been denied the classics." He pressed a few buttons on the front panel of the machine. "Now listen, and get ready to join the twentieth century."

After a moment a strange, thumping beat filled the room, followed by a high-pitched wail. Adam stared at the jukebox as he listened. The music didn't sound like anything he'd ever heard before. It throbbed in his chest, and he started to nod along with the beat.

"There," Michael said. "That's Elvis. You're getting it."

A deep male voice began to croon, singing about a hound dog. The singer's voice quavered and warbled, and suddenly Adam found the whole thing hilariously funny. He let out a loud burst of laughter.

"You like it?" Michael asked with a grin.

Adam sat down on one of the stools flanking the small coffee bar in the corner. "I love it," he said, twirling on the cushioned seat.

"Me too," Michael replied as he polished the jukebox's trim with the bottom of his T-shirt. "Although we should get some CDs from some people who are still actually alive, too. And I wouldn't mind having something to sit on besides those deflated beanbags upstairs. We'll have to hit some yard sales, see if we can find a sofa. Or maybe two recliners, like those guys on *Friends*."

Adam stopped twirling on the stool. Michael was talking about his place like it was Adam's as much as his. "Ray gave this place to *you*."

Michael shrugged. "If he'd known about you, he would have given it to both of us," he said. "We're from the same *planet*, you know? It's like we're family."

Family. Adam had seen pictures of families in those baby books Valenti had given him. But he'd never thought . . . He'd known they weren't for him.

"Thanks," Adam mumbled. It seemed the wrong thing to say, like there should be a better word.

"You know what the best part of having you live here is?" Michael asked. His tone was light, but Adam could see the emotion in his eyes.

"What?" Adam asked.

"You have to help clean." Michael handed him a broom, and Adam began sweeping shards of broken glass from the display cases into a small pile. Suddenly sweeping was an absurdly fun activity.

The door opened, and Maria stepped in, followed by Max and Isabel. "The cleanup crew is here!" Maria announced. Then she looked around the room. "And apparently we're extremely late. You guys have done a ton already."

"It's Adam," Michael claimed. "He tears into cleaning like he enjoys it."

"I do," Adam insisted.

"Whatever," Michael replied with a laugh.

Adam looked up just as Liz walked into the room, and his breath caught in his throat. She was wearing a red T-shirt that made her dark skin seem like it was lit from inside. Adam's face got hot, and he quickly turned away. He didn't want her or Max to catch him staring. Staring and smiling.

"I have to agree with Adam," Isabel said. "You guys know how I feel about clutter."

"No! You?" Maria asked. "Miss Anal USA?"

Isabel rolled her eyes but smiled. She pushed up the sleeves of her blue sweater. "So where can I start?"

"I'll take the alien autopsy section," Liz offered. "But first you have to tell me the truth. Those things in the jars aren't real aliens, are they?"

"They look like chicken embryos to me," Max said. "And I think that purple 'alien lungs' jar is nothing but a plastic bag floating in Jell-O."

"Ray was a sick puppy," Isabel said affectionately. She began to reorganize the moon rock display.

"Anyone want to join me?" Liz asked. Adam was about to drop the broom and volunteer, but Max beat him to it.

"I'm there," Max said, placing his hand on the small of Liz's back. Adam stared at Max's fingers, wishing they were his.

"The science geeks head for the biology display," Maria said with a laugh. "Shocker."

Adam gripped the broom handle hard and started sweeping with a vengeance. He might not have figured everything out about life aboveground, but Liz had made it very clear that Max was the only guy allowed to touch her. Adam had to remember that . . . no matter how beautiful she was or how amazing the sight of her made him feel.

FOUR

Adam stepped back as Maria hung the last grainy, black-and-white picture of a flying saucer on the wall, moving her hips to the music pounding from the jukebox.

"It looks straight to me," Adam said, squinting as he tried to keep from laughing at Maria's bizarre dance moves.

"Good," she said, slapping her hands together. She turned around and addressed the room. "So, we've wasted enough time on housekeeping. How are we going to get Alex back?"

Adam glanced around at the blank faces of his friends, knowing his expression reflected theirs exactly.

"We could find the ship," Isabel said finally, hopping onto a stool.

"How, brainiac?" Michael asked. "We have no idea who took it . . . or even how they managed to move something so big."

"Yeah, it might take some time to track down the ship," Max added. "A long time. I'm not saying we shouldn't look for it, but we need to think of an alternate way of bringing Alex home. The sooner the better."

"So what's plan B?" Liz asked.

"That's the problem," Max said. "We're currently plan B–less."

"Comforting," Isabel muttered.

"Unfortunately, we can't rely on the collective consciousness for help," Max said. He closed the glass door of a display case. "I'm not sure how long it will take for them to recover from opening the last wormhole, but I got the impression that it would be a few months, at least. So that's out."

"Wait, you connected to the consciousness?" Liz asked, paling. "When?"

Max paused and looked quickly around the room, not really focusing on anyone. "Last night," he said quietly.

Isabel jumped off the stool and grabbed his wrist. "Why didn't you *tell* us?" she asked. "How's Alex? Did they say anything about him?"

"He's . . . fine," Max said, shoving his hands in the front pockets of his jeans as his eyes flicked from one face to the next. "Alex is fine. But we still have to get him out of there."

"Well, *obviously*," Isabel said, crossing her arms over her chest. "But at least he's okay."

"Yeah . . . so . . . ," Max said.

Adam had the feeling there was something that Max wasn't telling them. His aura hadn't changed much, but there were a few minute flecks of oily yellow-green marring the rich jade.

"Wait a minute! If we all connected, could we open a wormhole ourselves?" Maria asked.

"Doubtful," Michael said. He walked over to the small sink behind the counter and started rinsing rags. "It takes a huge amount of power. . . . Right, Max?"

Max sighed, staring at the floor. "It was a struggle even with the whole consciousness working hard at it," he confirmed, running a hand over his blond hair.

"Well, what about the Stone of Midnight?" Liz asked. "Isn't that what that Stone is, really . . . a huge source of power?"

Wow, she's amazing, Adam thought as she brushed a stray strand of hair from her cheek. He wasn't able to stop the weird turmoil she caused inside him. Being near her made his mouth dry and his palms sweaty. Adam kept losing track of the discussion because his attention always seemed to return to Liz . . . and not to what she was saying, either. There was something about her warm, amber aura that made him feel both thrilled and queasy and made his knees weak.

"I don't think using the Stone is the best idea," Maria said. "I still see those bounty hunters in my nightmares."

The words *bounty hunters* got Adam's full attention. "The bounty hunters got sucked through the wormhole with Alex, though," he reminded everyone.

Not that any of them could have forgotten the sight of those two creatures getting pulled into the vortex, their tentacle-lined mouths open wide.

"You're right," Michael answered. "But we don't know how many bounty hunters were tracking the use of the Stōne's power for DuPris. DuPris could have a whole battalion of them out there."

A tiny shudder crossed Liz's body. Max moved closer to her and slid his arm around her shoulders.

Get off her. The thought blasted through Adam's mind, and he reminded himself for the billionth time that he actually liked Max and that Liz actually loved the guy.

"It's Alex. It's worth the risk of using the Stone," Isabel said.

"Agreed," Michael said. He turned away from the sink and leaned on the counter.

Max cleared his throat. "I hate to be the voice of reason here, but—"

"You do not," Isabel interrupted. "You live to be the voice of reason."

Everybody laughed, and Adam couldn't help noticing Liz's happy, musical sound. He wanted to hear it as much as possible. He wanted to be the one to make her laugh.

Something was definitely wrong with him.

"You were saying?" Liz asked Max.

"Before I was so *rudely* interrupted," Max continued with a smirk at his sister. "Yeah, maybe we could use the Stone. But we don't have it. DuPris does. And we have no idea where he is."

Adam felt a chill. Max was right. DuPris could teleport—he could be anywhere. He could be halfway around the world . . . although that concept was a bit fuzzy to Adam, who had only taken his first steps outside a few weeks ago. Still, he understood the distance enough to know that DuPris could be far, far away. Unreachable.

Or he could be right nearby, Adam realized, hugging himself to ward off the wave of ice that had invaded his body. DuPris, with all his poisonous hatred, could be right here in Roswell, with someone else's face.

Michael could at least have the decency to look dumpy sometimes, Maria thought. It would make being around him a little easier.

She watched him out of the corner of her eye as he drove Ray's car along the boring stretch of Route 285 north toward Albuquerque. Michael had decided to check out the old ranch house in the desert where they'd had the showdown with DuPris. It was possible, if unlikely, that DuPris was holing up there, using the ranch house as a base. If they found DuPris, they'd find the Stone.

Maria stared out the window at a reddish tan ridge of rock that ran along the highway, jutting up from the desert in the distance. Like a wall, Maria thought. Like the wall that stood between her and Michael now.

Which was the reason she had volunteered to keep him company. She had to see if she could fix the mess that lay between them.

They rode in silence. Usually Maria would be chatting to fill the chasm of quiet that separated them, but she and Michael had always talked so easily before. . . .

Before she told him she loved him.

Oh, that was a great idea, Maria thought glumly. You told him how you feel about him, and now as punishment you have to sit in silence forever.

Maria peeked at him again. He was staring straight out the windshield, his mouth and eyes grim with concentration. What's he concentrating on? she wondered. Driving? DuPris? Cameron? Keeping me shut out of his life?

Say something, Maria ordered herself as he reached a junction and turned off Route 285 to Route 60 west. This is your Michael. Just talk to him. Say anything!

"Uh . . . ," Michael said suddenly. He glanced at Maria and gave her a weak smile. "So . . ."

"Yeah?" Maria prompted. Talk to me! she screamed at him in her head. Can't you see I'm dying over here?

"Isabel seems really focused on getting Alex back," Michael said. "I guess she misses him after all. More than I thought she would."

"Why?" Maria shot back, more sharply than

she'd intended. "I'm not surprised. Alex is a great guy. Of course she misses him. We all miss him."

"Yeah, but that's not the kind of missing . . . ," Michael began. He adjusted his hands on the steering wheel. "Forget it."

Maria slumped back into the car seat. Isabel. Michael would have to mention her name, wouldn't he? Maria knew that Michael and Isabel had decided just to be friends, but hearing her name had made Maria remember the disgustingly embarrassing scene in which she'd tried to force Michael to choose between them.

He'd chosen Cameron instead. It had been one of the most humiliating, devastating moments in Maria's whole life.

Feeling more depressed now than when they'd started the trip, Maria turned to face the window as Michael pulled up in front of the ramshackle ranch house.

"What do we do now?" Maria asked.

"Have a look around," Michael said. "Ready?"

"As I'll ever be," Maria answered.

Together they walked up to the house. Maria found herself tiptoeing across the dirt yard, even though she knew it was impossible to sneak up on DuPris. At the front door Michael took a deep breath and turned the knob. The door swung open, and they both froze.

Nothing.

"He's not here," Michael said, stepping inside. Maria followed. The air smelled stale, like no one had walked through to circulate it in over a week. The large front room echoed with emptiness.

"I don't think he ever came back to this place," Maria said.

"I'm sorry for dragging you out here," Michael said. "This was a total waste of time."

Maria wandered farther into the room. She could still so easily picture the horrible scene that had taken place there, the sense of complete powerlessness, of being under DuPris's control.

She stopped over the spot where DuPris had kept her frozen in place.

What a good little bunny you are, DuPris had murmured into her ear. Her terror at that moment had been overwhelming, and even recalling it now made her shiver. *I wonder what thoughts bunnies are capable of having. . . .*

And then he'd plucked an image from her mind—an image of herself hoping to kiss Michael. Amused, DuPris had forced Maria to walk over to Michael and put her arms around him. It was the worst violation she'd ever experienced. At least touching Michael had allowed Maria to make a connection to him, which had broken DuPris's hold over them.

Now it seemed a total mystery how she'd made that deep connection with Michael. She couldn't even think of anything to *say* to him anymore—never mind a union of their auras.

Suddenly all of it—the gulf between her and Michael, DuPris getting away, Alex exiled to another galaxy—it was all too much for Maria to handle. She took a deep breath and burst into hot, uncontrollable sobs.

This was the last place she wanted to have a meltdown. Here. In front of him.

"Maria, don't," Michael said, his voice soft and full of concern.

She wheeled around to face him, tears trailing down her face. She rubbed them away and struggled to get a grip, but fresh tears kept streaming down her cheeks. "How . . . how are we ever going to get . . . Alex back?" she choked out. "Everything's against us! Nothing . . . nothing . . . nothing's going right."

"Maria, you—"

"No!" she shouted at him. "Don't 'Maria' me! You don't even have the decency . . . the common *decency* . . . to look dumpy sometimes!"

"What?" Michael demanded.

Maria turned away. "It doesn't matter," she wailed. "Nothing matters. Alex is gone. DuPris has the Stone. And you . . ."

And you don't love me.

But Maria couldn't say that. She could never say that.

Instead she spun around and ran out the door. She bolted over to the car, jumped in, and slammed the door. She just wanted to be home. She just wanted to be away from Michael. She never thought she'd feel that way, but she did.

After a long moment Maria heard Michael climb behind the wheel. He didn't say anything, just wrapped his arms around her. His aura wrapped around hers with all the comfort of a towel straight out of the dryer.

"I just feel so awful . . . about everything," she said, pressing her face into his shoulder.

"I know," he said. "I do, too."

"What are we going to do?" she asked, her voice muffled.

Michael let out a long sigh. "I don't know."

He held her for a few minutes, rocking her until her tears stopped. Then he pulled away, holding her shoulders.

"You know what I've got?" Michael asked.

Maria wiped her nose with the back of her hand. "Uh-uh," she said.

He dug into his pocket and pulled out a small cloth satchel tied with a dark red ribbon. He waved it in front of her face. "Remember this?"

Maria's heart skipped a beat. It was the aroma-therapy satchel she'd made for him. She couldn't believe he carried it with him.

"Take it," Michael said.

Maria held the little satchel up to her nose. The smell of rose petals, eucalyptus, and pine needles filled her sinuses, clearing them with the strong fragrance. She held on to the satchel for a few moments, inhaling deeply. Those were three of her favorite scents in the world.

"Better?" Michael asked.

Maria nodded, giving him a smile that felt like it could break into pieces any second.

"Thanks," she said.

"No," Michael said, putting his arm around her. "Thank you. Somebody's got to let themselves feel all this crap we're going through, and nobody can do it better than you."

And all of a sudden Maria didn't want to be anywhere but where she was.

Michael did love her. Not the way she dreamed of him loving her. But still.

Isabel winced as she watched a look of pain cross Adam's face.

She, Adam, and Max were up in Ray's apartment—Michael's apartment—and Max had connected to Adam, trying to find out if Adam had any buried memories of the time DuPris had been in control of his body.

Adam's face screwed up in pain again, and Isabel shut her eyes. After Max was done with Adam, she was next. Isabel knew it was important, even crucial, but she was looking forward to it like a trip to the dentist.

When Isabel heard Max sigh, she opened her eyes again. Max and Adam were sitting beside each other on Michael's bed, and Adam was rubbing his forehead.

"Anything?" Isabel asked.

"Zilch," Max said. "Except that Adam's interesting in there. He's got powers I've never even *heard* of."

Adam smiled. "I've just been practicing longer," he said.

"Okay, Izzy, it's your turn," Max said.

Adam hopped up and headed downstairs. "I'm going to go see what Liz is doing," he said.

Isabel took his seat, her heart pounding with apprehension.

"Ready?" Max asked.

"Sure," Isabel answered, trying to sound calm, even though she knew Max was the last person on earth she could fool. But he didn't call her on her false bravery. He simply took her hand gently, and they were instantly connected.

Isabel felt Max's emerald green energy mingling with her own rich purple, and they headed for Isabel's memory centers. *Their* memory center. The connection between them was more than a simple attachment—it was a true sharing of souls.

The first image they uncovered was completely familiar. She was shopping at Victoria's Secret for something that would make Michael's mouth water.

She'd taken the bus back to the museum, and then DuPris had used her to hurt Michael. Isabel watched in shock as the memory replayed in their mind. DuPris had made her betray one of her best friends. The very idea of it filled her with fury.

Max sent soothing images of family dinners with their parents at her until she calmed down. When Isabel had relaxed, she sensed Max asking her if she was ready to continue. Yes, she was ready. Go for it.

Her brother dug deeper, unleashing a torrent of memories of her time under DuPris's control. Isabel transformed into a child, hiding out with DuPris at the ranch. DuPris touching her face in the most loathsome way. DuPris laughing as Isabel raged against his hold on her. Isabel using her powers to fling Max against a wall.

There had to be something in her that would let them find DuPris. How she would love to rip out his lungs and use them as bagpipes!

Max soothed her again, willing her to stay calm. They'd learn nothing if she broke concentration.

Then Max poked at a dark, unformed image. Isabel concentrated on the black memory, curious despite her fear of what it might contain. There was no visual to it, only a sound . . . the sound of a car . . . and the smell of exhaust and oil.

Max encouraged her to replay the memory. DuPris had locked her in the trunk of his car. She'd felt so claustrophobic and terrified. Then DuPris opened the trunk, but the recollection remained hazy and dim.

DuPris was making her walk through the darkness. Isabel stumbled over loose rocks and held on to a guide rope to assist herself down the cavern path.

Cavern?

Yes, Isabel realized with a rush of excitement. They were in a cave. Her eyes were adjusting, and she'd seen stalactites, stalagmites . . . swooping bats. What cave was it? She just had to remember a little more, notice a landmark—

But then the memory went black. Something had knocked her out.

Max let go of Isabel's hand. "Do you have any idea where that cave was?" he asked.

"Not a clue," Isabel said, her mind still reeling. "But we have to figure it out."

"There are a million caves like that around here," Max said, rubbing his forehead.

Isabel grabbed his hand and looked him directly in the eye. "I know it's practically hopeless," she said. "But it's the only chance we've got to save Alex."

I should have thought of coming here myself, Liz thought as she climbed through the first-floor office window of the *Astral Projector,* the tabloid newspaper DuPris had published before he disappeared. She fell through the window and landed on the floor at Adam's feet.

Adam had found a copy of the *Astral Projector,* with its pages of doctored photographs of alien encounters, in Ray's museum. Apparently Ray subscribed—probably to give himself a good laugh every month. As soon as Liz explained to Adam what the newspaper was, he'd been sure the tabloid's office was the perfect place to search for clues to DuPris's whereabouts. And he didn't want to wait for Max and Isabel to be done upstairs.

Liz didn't want to wait, either. She was glad to have something to do. Anything that might lead to getting Alex back home.

"Where should we start?" Adam asked.

"You take the desk," Liz said as she looked around the dark office. "I'll go through DuPris's file cabinet." She shut the blinds and flicked on the overhead light.

Adam started rifling through the desk, and Liz opened the top drawer of the file cabinet, marked Abyss–Humidity. She pulled out the first file and scanned it.

"Abyss" turned out to be a bunch of articles about a hole in Colorado that led to the center of the earth, where an alien race had built a civilization. This was according to some questionable sources that DuPris had interviewed. It sounded insane to Liz, but then the *Astral Projector's* stock-in-trade wasn't exactly reality. DuPris had just used the newspaper as a cover for his investigation of Michael, Isabel, and Max and his search for the Stone of

Midnight. Liz was amazed that he'd kept records at all.

Diligently Liz skimmed every article in the drawer, even though there were hundreds of them. She didn't want to miss anything that might help Alex. By the time she reached the file titled Humidity, she was struggling to contain her giggles over the ridiculousness of it all. "Humidity" was an article about how aliens from some planet called Neutron-6 needed to keep their skin moist at all times or they'd shrivel up like worms on the sidewalk after it rained.

"The scary thing is that people believe this stuff," Liz muttered to herself as she replaced the file. She had just closed the top drawer of the filing cabinet when she heard footsteps in the hallway outside the office.

The hair on Liz's arms rose as the doorknob started to turn. She glanced at Adam, and his eyes were wide with fear.

"Quick!" Liz hissed. "Under the desk!"

A second later the two of them were smashed together in the small space in front of DuPris's desk chair. "The light," Adam whispered as the door creaked open.

Liz squeezed her eyes shut. There was nothing to do about it now.

Liz strained her back until it hurt and peered under the metal edge of the desk. She stretched and managed to glimpse a pair of sensible shoes and a set of wheels on a cart. An odor of disinfectant wafted through the room.

It was the cleaning service. Liz's heart calmed in her chest. Although it still wouldn't be good to be discovered, she'd take the maid over DuPris any day.

"Always leaving the light on," the cleaning woman mumbled to herself.

As the cleaning lady emptied a garbage can near the door, Liz started to become very aware of Adam's arm lying across her stomach and his cheek pressed up against her shoulder. She could feel his heart beating . . . and it was thumping pretty rapidly, too.

She glanced at his face, and in the moment before he looked away, she saw that he was staring at her with wide, amazed eyes. Liz tried to shift away, but the space under the desk wasn't exactly roomy.

Adam's obvious crush on her had always seemed kind of sweet . . . from a distance. But up close, it was making her nervous and tense. Liz held her body taut, trying to prevent any skin contact whatsoever, trying to send out an anti-attraction vibe. She listened to Adam's ragged breathing and felt her face flush.

Liz stole a peek at Adam again. It wasn't that he wasn't cute—quite the contrary. He was muscular and sleek. But Adam wasn't Max, and that was that.

The cleaning woman finally left, shutting off the light and closing the door behind her. Liz scrambled out from under the desk as fast as she could and brushed herself off. The darkness in the office seemed far too intimate, so Liz hurried to turn the overhead light back on.

Adam didn't emerge for another minute, lingering as if he'd hoped their uncomfortable situation didn't have to end. He smiled awkwardly at her as he climbed to his feet.

Liz needed to take control before Adam said or, even worse, *did* something they'd all regret later. "Okay," she said. "Back to work."

"I'm done with the desk," Adam said. He sounded almost remorseful, as if he'd done something wrong. As maybe he had . . . in his imagination. Liz cut that thought off before her *own* imagination started supplying details.

"Then check out DuPris's bookshelf," Liz ordered. "Look inside the books, too, in case he's hidden something inside one of them."

Liz returned to the file cabinet, and by the time she was halfway through the third drawer, she had a monster crick in her neck. As she reached deep into the drawer to pull the files and condense them so they opened more easily, her finger grazed something along the side of the drawer. Liz yanked her hand away. "Ow," she muttered. She stuck her index finger into her mouth, tasting the coppery flavor of her own blood. Paper cut.

But what had she cut her finger on?

With her other hand Liz reached into the space

between the hanging files and the side of the drawer. And found a manila folder that had been inserted into that space sideways.

She pulled it out, her hand shaking with excitement. It could be a folder that had been dropped there accidentally, or it could be something DuPris hadn't wanted to be easily found. . . .

Liz opened the folder. It contained a single photo.

A photo of a middle-aged guy in a military uniform shaking hands with Sheriff Valenti. Both men were smiling at the camera.

With a jolt Liz realized that she recognized the man in the uniform.

It was Mr. Manes.

Alex's father.

Liz's stomach lurched.

This doesn't have to mean anything, she told herself as she stared at the picture. Alex's dad is retired air force, and Valenti was the town sheriff. There could be hundreds of reasons why they were hanging out. It could be some kind of macho-guy barbecue.

But the scene in the picture didn't look like it was taking place at a barbecue. It looked like an office. Valenti's office at the Clean Slate compound, to be exact.

Liz's heart dropped to the floor. It can't be, she thought. But what other explanation is there?

If Alex's father was at the secret compound, he had to be a member of Project Clean Slate, too.

FIVE

Maria tried to open the front door to her house as quietly as humanly possible, but she wasn't doing a great job. The keys seemed to be making an incredibly loud jangling racket as she unlocked the door. It was late—very, very late. She'd still been on the road back from the ranch house with Michael at nine, and that was hours ago.

Not that it really mattered. Her mom was probably out somewhere wearing clothes that were way too tight for someone her age.

Maria stepped into the house and saw her ten-year-old brother, Kevin, standing on the stairs in his pajamas.

"You are in so much trouble," he whispered, his mouth exaggerating the shape of his words.

"Why?" Maria whispered back. "Is Mom—"

"Maria, is that you?" her mother called from the living room.

As Maria groaned, Kevin zipped back up the stairs. Little weasel, Maria thought without any real malice. Her little brother was an expert at getting out of the line of fire, a skill she wished she possessed.

Maria turned to see her mother swooping toward her across the foyer, a worried look on her face. She was wearing regular mom clothes—sweatshirt and jeans. Not a good sign.

And right beside her was Sheriff Kasey Dodson. A very bad sign.

For a second Maria thought her heart, trailing her entire circulatory system, was going to leap out of the top of her skull. Sure, she was late, but so late that her mom called the *police* on her?

Or what if Sheriff Dodson was Clean Slate, like Liz and Max suspected? What if she knew who Maria's friends were and had come there to interrogate her?

"Where have you *been?*" Maria's mother demanded. "It's after eleven, and I got no call, no note. Not acceptable."

"I was just over at Liz's," Maria lied quickly.

She couldn't say she'd gone on a road trip with a guy—even Michael. Her mother would freak, and mentioning him in front of the sheriff seemed like a bad idea—just in case she did know who Michael, Max, Isabel, and Adam really were.

"We got sucked into a late movie and lost track of the time. It was some old horror flick about giant ants." Maria knew that she ranked high on the list of the world's worst liars, but she could fool her mother if it was really necessary. Sheriff Dodson was another story. Maria glanced at the new sheriff to see how she was taking Maria's alibi.

72

There was a funny, small smile playing on Sheriff Dodson's lips, which could have been skepticism. But it was quickly replaced by a grim frown.

"You should call if you're out later than you expected," the sheriff advised sternly. "It's not fair to worry your mother when picking up the phone only takes a minute."

Maria blinked, turning over the sheriff's words, searching for any hidden meaning. She came up with nothing. The sheriff's statement seemed clean.

"You're so right," Maria told Sheriff Dodson, then turned to face her mother. "I'm sorry, Mom. I should have called."

"Next time, okay?" her mother replied.

"I will."

Maria's mother let out a long sigh. "Would everyone like some tea?" she asked. "I even have some with caffeine that Maria doesn't know about."

"Mom, you promised to cut out the stimulants," Maria protested.

"Sounds great, Mimi, but I can't," Sheriff Dodson interrupted, glancing at Maria. "If everything's okay here now, I've got to get home to Julie. If she wakes up and finds I'm not there . . . Well, it wouldn't be good."

Maria stared at the sheriff in confusion. Her mother's first name was Margaret, and only her close friends called her Mimi. What was going on? Why were her mother and Sheriff Dodson suddenly acting all buddy-buddy? And who was Julie?

"Some other time," Mrs. DeLuca said. "And thanks, Kasey, for helping me out tonight."

"No problem," Sheriff Dodson said as she headed toward the door. "You know where to find me if you need anything."

She walked out. It wasn't until after she closed the door behind her that Maria felt her heart rate begin to slow. Even though the sheriff hadn't said one word that seemed suspicious, Maria still felt like she'd just had a close call.

Mrs. DeLuca put her hand on Maria's shoulder. "I could still make tea—some of your stuff," she said. "I could use a cup myself. Want any?"

"Sure," Maria said.

She followed her mother into the kitchen and took two teacups out of the cabinet. "Who's Julie?" Maria asked.

"Kasey's daughter," Mrs. DeLuca replied. She filled a teakettle with water at the sink. "That's why she came over this evening. Tonight was my night to host my MWP group, remember? We had a good turnout."

MWP stood for Mothers Without Partners, a support group Maria's mother had joined after the divorce. So Dodson's being here really had nothing to do with Maria—probably.

Maria took a deep breath. "That's great!" she said with a way-too-big smile.

"Kasey stayed after the meeting and helped me clean up," Maria's mother said. She put the kettle on the stove and turned on the burner. "Then she hung around to keep me company while I waited up for you."

"I didn't mean to make you worry," Maria said as she sat down at the kitchen table.

Mrs. DeLuca sat down across from Maria and smiled. "All's well that ends well, right?" she said. "Just call next time."

"I will," Maria promised. And she would because she had no wish to come home ever again and find the sheriff in her house.

Maybe I'm just being paranoid, she thought. But the whole story about Sheriff Dodson just happening to hang around tonight seems a little too convenient. What if she's part of Clean Slate and just using Mom to keep an eye on me?

Yeah, Maria was being paranoid.

But sometimes a healthy dose of paranoia could keep you alive.

"You're not going to believe this," Max said as Michael pulled himself into Max's bedroom through the window.

"Sounds big," Michael said, brushing off the front of his black T-shirt.

"It's huge," Max responded, his blue eyes wide. "Liz and Adam broke into DuPris's office."

Michael's face went slack. "They did *what?*" he demanded. "Do they have a death wish or something?"

"That's not even half of it," Max said, plopping down on the edge of his bed. He leaned forward, resting his elbows on his knees and clasping his hands in front of him. He looked up at Michael, hoping he wasn't going to lose it when he heard the news.

"What is it?" Michael asked.

"They found a picture of Valenti in his office at the compound," Max said. He took a deep breath.

"And?" Michael prompted.

"And he was shaking hands with Alex's dad."

Michael just looked at Max for a moment. Then he slowly lowered himself onto the desk chair. "The Major is Clean Slate."

It was a statement, not a question, but Max felt the need to answer it, anyway.

"We don't know that for sure," he said. "It could mean nothing."

"But it could mean something," Michael said, his gray eyes flashing. "If he's Clean Slate, he's already out for our blood, and if he finds out we're responsible for Alex's disappearance . . ."

Max's stomach twisted uncomfortably, and he found himself staring at the carpet. *We're responsible.* There should have been some way to tell the difference between Alex and DuPris while the wormhole was open. Even though Alex had been molecularly altered to resemble DuPris, Max still should have been able to tell them apart somehow—

"It was an accident," Michael said. "I can feel you getting your boxers in a bunch over there. Stop it, Max. How many times do we have to tell you it wasn't your fault? You were *tricked*. We all were. I was just thinking that any Clean Slate agent would *assume* it was us."

Max nodded, but he wasn't totally convinced. He knew he was going to feel guilty until Alex was back where he belonged. On earth.

"So . . . what do we do about the Major?" Max asked, changing the subject.

"Avoid him like the plague?" Michael suggested.

"There's still a possibility that he has nothing to do with anything," Max said. "I need more proof than a photo Liz found in *DuPris's* file cabinet. It's not like the *Astral Projector* ever printed a photo that wasn't doctored."

"Good point," Michael said. "We'll just keep an eye on him . . . from afar."

"And act cool if we run into him," Max added.

"Maybe you can *act* cool," Michael said, smiling. "But you're never going to *be* cool, geek."

"Dork," Max replied.

"I don't have to take this abuse," Michael said, pushing himself out of his chair. "I'm outta here."

"So soon?"

"Yeah," Michael said. He shook his new keys

with a grin. "I want to go kick back at Ray's place, now that it's my place. Jealous?"

Max rolled his eyes. "Insanely," he answered. "Later."

"Peace out," Michael joked, climbing through the window.

When he was gone, Max lay back in bed and decided to distract himself with some mindless TV. He started surfing channels and stopped on a cooking show, but the combinations of ingredients didn't appeal to him. Humans just never mixed sweets and spicy foods for some reason. Like a hamburger covered in applesauce. Mmm.

The collective consciousness agreed with him. A ripple of approving images entered the back of Max's mind. Yes, they concurred. They loved fried meat and tangy fruit together. One of the beings gave Max a taste of a favorite dish, and he could feel the juices running down his throat. Awesome.

Then he realized he hadn't tried to connect to the consciousness at all.

Was it going to be like this for the rest of his life? The idea that the collective consciousness would always be peering over his metaphoric shoulder gave Max the creeps. Will the connection keep getting stronger? Max wondered. Even when I'm not trying to connect?

He sat up in bed and rubbed his eyes. Maybe he should cut back on the amount of time he spent willingly making a full connection to the consciousness. Maybe that would stop or slow down the automatic linking.

But if I do that, Max thought, then how can I keep tabs on how Alex is doing? I've got to keep everybody calm about Alex.

Max closed his eyes. That's what he should be doing right now—checking up on Alex. No matter how it affected Max, making sure Alex was safe was his number-one priority.

With a deep breath Max opened himself up to the full force of the collective consciousness and sank into the ocean of interconnected auras. Like he was floating in a warm bath, Max felt buoyed up by the network of souls. Then he became absorbed by them, one among the multitudes.

Alex? he sent out, along with an image of his redheaded friend laughing at one of his own jokes. How's Alex?

Most of the responses Max received in return were positive—friendly replies, from beings who had begun to adjust to Alex living among them.

Then Max bumped into an aura he recognized.

It was Alex himself. And he was terrified out of his mind.

Max received an image from Alex of pure fear, of shadowy threatening presences, of misery and loneliness. There was no place for Alex to relax or rest. He was constantly on the run. Running for his life.

What is it? Max sent out frantically. *Alex, what's wrong? What are you running from?*

But before Alex could reply, another being took his place—an unfriendly entity who blasted Max with images of fire and destruction. Max recoiled . . . and lost track of Alex in the whirlwind of auras.

He thrust himself into the storm, struggling to hold on to Alex's signature energy, but to no avail. The angry being had blocked Alex from further communication.

How can I get him home if you won't even let me talk to him? We want the same thing—we both want Alex back on earth! He knew he wasn't getting his message across. His reasoning was too hard to express in images.

Max received no response, so he decided to shout directly to Alex.

Alex, he sent, *Alex, if you can hear me, we're trying to bring you back! We all miss you, and we want you to come home! I promise . . . I promise we will find a way to get you here where you belong!*

Max disconnected from the full force of the collective consciousness and sat up on his bed, gasping for breath. What was going on? Where had all that anger come from?

It made Max sick to think of Alex out there, alone and scared. But all Max could do was hope that most of the consciousness was still trying to understand and that those beings would keep his friend safe.

*   *   *

Liz looked incredible today, Adam thought. He lay on the living-room floor and let his mind drift back to the scene in the *Astral Projector* office. Liz under the desk with him. Her soft, sweet-smelling body pressed up against his. Her lips so close, he could have kissed her. . . .

With a groan Adam flipped over and buried his face in one of the flat beanbags. He wished it was time for his short sleep period because then he wouldn't be lost in thinking about Liz. Probably.

I wonder if she dreams about me, Adam thought. Right, like that was even possible. But still, maybe he should go dream walking and check out her dream orb. He'd give anything to see what Liz dreamed about.

No, Adam told himself. It would violate her privacy. And what right did he have thinking about her so much, anyway? She was with Max. They were boyfriend and girlfriend. Adam was nothing to her. Nothing special, anyhow.

And Max had been so great to him. They all had.

So Adam definitely shouldn't peek into Liz's dream orb.

Definitely.

But nothing was stopping him from dream walking elsewhere. Even when he'd been confined to the compound, dream walking had allowed him a little taste of freedom. He could experience the whole world in dreams.

And if he stopped by Liz's dream—just stopped by to look at it from the outside—who would that hurt?

Nobody.

Adam flipped over on his back and closed his eyes. He let a wave of calm creep up his body, starting with his toes. When the current of relaxation reached his head, Adam opened his eyes on the dream plane. He was surrounded by billions of glowing spheres, a chaotic field of bubbles stretching into the distance. Brilliant colors swirled on the surfaces of the spheres, and each gave off a pure note so rich, it barely translated as sound. Adam felt the music deeply more than just heard it—this was a music all the senses had to share.

Each bubble was attached to a dreamer. Adam whistled softly, concentrating on picturing Liz. Sure enough, she was asleep, and her dream sphere floated toward Adam's summons. He held the whistled note until Liz's sphere spun close enough for him to see inside.

What he saw sent a jolt through him. Liz was having a nightmare.

Something was chasing her through her house. She ran up the stairs, her eyes wide with terror, as she searched for someplace to hide. The walls contracted until they were as narrow as tunnels. A thick blue fog filled the stairwell, making it hard for Liz to see who was chasing her and making it even harder for her to escape.

Adam placed his open hands around the orb, willing the sphere to expand until the figures inside were life-size.

Liz was in a bedroom now, surrounded by the fog, backing up against the headboard of the bed. Out reached a pair of hands and grabbed Liz by the throat. She saw its face for the first time, and Adam saw it, too. The thing . . . the thing was Liz. Another Liz. With lips and eyes sewn shut with thick black thread.

Adam had seen enough. He charged inside her dream orb. He grabbed the creature, and instantly it turned to dust. Then he took Liz by the hand and switched the scene to someplace Liz would feel safe—the ground floor of the UFO museum.

"Get it away! Get it away!" Liz screamed.

"It's gone," Adam said soothingly. "Would you like to hear some music?"

Still shaken, Liz nodded. Adam pressed a button on the jukebox. The music that poured out was smooth and slow, with a high, beautiful melody.

"That's nice," Liz said. She began to sway back and forth. And then she smiled at him, dimpling her left cheek.

A strong pang of guilt coursed through Adam. Was this okay, him here with Liz? Max wouldn't care if they were just doing friendly stuff, right?

Yeah, Max definitely would have wanted Adam to take Liz out of that nightmare. Do something to take her mind off it. Like . . . like ask her to dance.

Adam held out his arms to her. "Would you—"

"Sure," Liz said. She smiled again, but her expression was different this time. It was less friendly and more . . . interesting.

Adam gulped as he stepped toward her, but she didn't seem nervous at all. Liz met his gaze, her brown eyes glowing with warmth. Then she was in his arms, his hands clasped at the small of her back. Her tender amber aura washed over his lemon yellow energy like the first streaks of a sunset.

He couldn't forget any of this moment. It was too precious. Adam took a second to memorize everything he was sensing. The supple feel of her body against his own. The heat of her hands on his shoulders. The soft brush of her hair against his cheek.

After all, if it wasn't a dream, he wouldn't have the chance to hold Liz like this. He might never have the opportunity again.

Not in the real world.

In the real world, they would always be just friends.

SIX

"How is anybody supposed to eat this?" Liz asked her friends, all of whom were seated around a long table in the school cafeteria. All her friends minus Alex, of course. And Adam. They still hadn't figured out a way to register him for school without every social services department in the country swooping down on him. So Adam hung out in Michael's apartment alone during the day.

Adam. Liz had woken up with an odd feeling about him this morning—a pleasant feeling, too. But she couldn't put her finger on where it came from.

"That's why I brought tuna fish," Maria said. "You couldn't pay me to eat this cafeteria garbage."

Michael looked at them with feigned shock. "What are you talking about?" he protested. He added extra pickles to the top of his slice of sausage pizza. "This is a gourmet meal."

"That is the most vile thing I've ever seen," Liz said, pointing at his lunch.

"Seriously," Isabel said. "You could have at least added some Sweet'n Low."

"Oh, yuck!" Maria said.

"Fine. More for me, then," Michael replied with a smile.

Liz smiled, too, but she was wondering why Max had been so quiet all lunch period. He hadn't joined in any of their joking around, and he hadn't even sat beside Liz at the table. Max was sitting on the other side of Isabel, across from Michael, lost in his thoughts. Drifting to . . . wherever.

"Max," Liz said. "Earth to Max."

He looked up at her, surprised. "Oh," he said, a faint blush coloring his cheeks. "Sorry. I was just thinking about the cave."

"Isabel's memory?" Maria asked.

Max nodded. "I've been racking my brain for any distinguishing factors, but so far . . . zilch, zip—"

"Nada," Isabel said. "Me too. It's all a blur. I wish I could remember it better, but—wait, scratch that. . . . I'm glad I don't remember. DuPris's a pig."

"What *do* you remember? Is it like your cave?" Maria asked, referring to the cave where Michael, Isabel, and Max had broken free of their incubation pods. They used it as their hideaway from the rest of the world and had brought Liz, Maria, and Alex there when they'd first started hanging out together. Now they often used it as a sort of crisis headquarters.

"You mean *our* cave?" Isabel said, looking at Liz and Maria meaningfully. Liz smiled at her. She knew it took a lot for Isabel to include her new friends in something so close to her heart. "DuPris's cave was a lot bigger," Isabel continued, "but it had all your basic stuff—stalagmites, stalactites, bats, darkness, the works. A cave."

"There are a million places like that in New Mexico." Michael groaned. "Max and I have been searching the desert for years, and we've only hit the smallest fraction of the caves out there."

"It doesn't even have to be in New Mexico," Liz added glumly. "DuPris can teleport, remember? He followed us back to the museum from the ranch house. And he took the bounty hunters along with him that time, so he could have transported Isabel and Adam, too."

"I remembered being in the back of a car," Isabel argued.

"He could have done that just to trick you," Michael pointed out. "So it would be harder for us to follow him . . . which it is."

The bell rang, signaling the end of lunch period.

Biology, Liz thought as she stood up. At least it was her favorite class of the day, and Max was in it with her. Maybe he wouldn't be so out of it if they were sitting next to each other, doing experiments together.

Liz said her good-byes, and she and Max headed out of the cafeteria toward the biology lab. When they were halfway down the hall, Liz nudged Max with her arm.

"You ready for today?" she asked. "We're playing matchmaker to a bunch of mutant fruit flies."

Max stopped short. "You know what?" he said. "I left my book in my locker. I'll catch up with you, okay?"

"Yeah . . . okay," Liz replied, but Max had already headed down the corridor.

With a sigh, Liz continued to the lab. He's just preoccupied, she told herself.

She made a detour for the drinking fountain by the trophy case. As she bent down, a strong hand grabbed her shoulder. Her first thought was that Max had come back for her. But no way would Max grab her so hard it *hurt*.

She spun around quickly. Kyle Valenti stood there, glaring at her. Sweat was trickling down his forehead from his hairline, and his pupils were like tiny black pinholes.

"What are you doing?" Liz asked, trying to keep her voice as light as possible. She shrugged her shoulder free. "Is there a problem?"

"Problem?" Kyle repeated. He laughed, but it came out more like a choked gasp. "Yeah, there's a problem! Why don't you tell me where my father is?"

His father. Suddenly Liz was overwhelmed by a rush of fear, pity, and confusion, and she had to fight to keep it all from showing on her face. Liz felt bad for Kyle—he had lost his dad. Sheriff Valenti was a horrible person, but Liz didn't even like to consider how she'd feel if her papa disappeared.

But how did he know she'd had anything to

do with Sheriff Valenti's disappearance? How much did he know?

"Your dad?" Liz asked, carefully maintaining a calm exterior. "What are you talking about?"

Kyle narrowed his eyes, half covering his shrunken pupils.

"I know you had something to do with it!" Kyle snapped. "You were snooping around my house that day—right before I saw him for the last time. You expect me to believe that's just a *coincidence?*"

"Kyle, I'm so sorry," Liz said as sincerely as she could manage. "But I honestly don't know where he is." She tried to push past him before he saw in her eyes that she was lying.

Kyle held on to her arm. "So then why were you in my house?" he demanded.

"Kyle, I already told you," Liz began with a nervous laugh, trying frantically to remember the explanation she and Maria had come up with when he'd found them there a week ago. "Maria . . . and I . . . were decorating all the football players' houses, just for a laugh—"

"Don't feed me that bull again!" Kyle yelled. "Is he dead? Did you *kill* him? Either tell me what you know, or—"

"Or what?" Liz asked, taking a step back.

"Or I'll—," Kyle began. He looked around the hallway. "I'll—"

Kyle suddenly turned and smashed his fist

through the plate glass of the trophy case beside them.

Liz jumped as shards of glass crashed to the floor. God, Kyle was out of his mind! He'd always been an idiot, but the sheriff's disappearance had sent him right over the edge. Liz winced as she saw blood oozing out of the cuts on Kyle's hand. For a moment she was so stunned, she couldn't even move.

"Security!" somebody called from down the corridor. Liz looked over to see Ms. Shaffer rushing toward them with the two burly security guys following close behind.

"What the hell's going on over here?" Ms. Shaffer took one look at the blood running down Kyle's wrist and the smashed trophy case and realized what had happened. "Kyle? Are you all right?"

"It's her!" Kyle shouted. "She did something to my father! She's in on it! She's in on it!"

Liz watched, stunned, as the security guards quickly led Kyle away. He kept shouting as they half pulled him out of sight around a corner. Liz's stomach clenched with a mixture of guilt, sympathy, and fear.

"Liz, what happened here?" Ms. Shaffer asked.

"Well . . . Kyle wanted to date me a few months ago, and I turned him down. He hasn't been too happy with me since then." She figured it was good to mix some truth into her story. "And just now? I don't really know what the deal was. Kyle started yelling something about his father. Some kind of family problem. I had no idea what he was talking about. And then he just snapped."

"Huh," Ms. Shaffer replied. "Strange. Very strange."

"You can say that again," Liz said. She scanned the principal's face for any sign of disbelief, but she seemed to buy Liz's story.

Ms. Shaffer touched Liz's arm lightly. "Are you all right?"

"Oh, I'm fine," Liz said. Only after the principal asked did she realize how fast her heart was beating. "Just a little shaken up." She took a deep breath. "Well, I guess I should get to class."

She took off down the hall, ordering herself not to break into a run. As soon as she turned the corner, Liz slumped against the wall.

Kyle knows, she thought. Kyle knows! Liz and her friends weren't responsible for Sheriff Valenti's death, but they were there when it happened. And DuPris had used Adam's body to do the dirty work. If Kyle suspected them and kept digging, Adam—and the rest of her friends—could be in a lot of trouble.

Liz pushed herself off the wall and walked to the water fountain on the other side of the hall. Kyle'd grabbed her before she got her drink. As she sipped, she forced herself to look at the situation rationally.

What, exactly, did Kyle know?

Enough to accuse her, but not anything more than that, she decided as she straightened up and continued down the hall and up the stairs. He had no proof of any kind. And his accusations were based on circumstantial evidence at best.

But did he know more than he was letting on?

Did he know about Project Clean Slate? Did the sheriff tell his son he was on Max, Isabel, and Michael's trail? Had Kyle ever hung out at the compound?

Maybe Kyle is the one who chased us through the desert, Liz thought, taking a deep breath. He was obviously off at the moment. It definitely could have been him.

Liz headed toward the lab, her mind reeling. If Kyle was the one who'd chased them, did that mean he'd somehow managed to move the ship, too?

Pausing outside the biology lab door, Liz took one more deep breath to steady herself. Kyle couldn't have moved the ship.

Not without a lot of help.

Somehow that wasn't a very comforting thought.

Isabel drove the Jeep through the suburban back streets of Roswell, heading for Alex's house. Max and Michael might have decided to leave Mr. Manes alone for the time being, but that didn't mean Isabel had to do the same.

Since Valenti died, Isabel had felt safe. Or at least *safer* than she'd ever felt before. The man who had haunted her nightmares for years was no more.

But apparently the maniac had friends right here in Roswell.

Isabel *had* to know if Alex's father was Clean Slate. Until she found out for sure, it would drive her crazy. The whole idea that the Major could belong to an agency that seemed dedicated to her personal eradication made her feel like she was itching all over her body. She'd met him. She'd had dinner at his table.

What if Alex's dad *is* Clean Slate and he's the one who removed the ship? Isabel wondered as she turned up the Maneses' driveway. He could be jeopardizing Alex's only chance to get home . . . and not even know it.

Isabel had no idea what she would do if she discovered the Major was part of the same horrible organization as Valenti, but she'd think of something. She'd have to. No matter what it took, she couldn't allow Alex's own father to get in the way of saving him.

No matter what it took.

Isabel killed the engine. She'd risk anything to get Alex home safely. Even snoop around in the house of a man whose mission in life could be tracking Isabel down, locking her away, experimenting on her, and then . . .

Isabel ordered herself not to complete the thought. She climbed out of the Jeep and headed up to the front door. This is for Alex, she repeated in her head. Think of Alex.

Isabel was unprepared to have Mrs. Manes answer the doorbell. She'd been ready to flirt with the

Major and sweet-talk him into letting her look around. Isabel liked Mrs. Manes, but she had no idea what Alex might have told his mother about their breakup. With his dad, she could have been sure that Alex hadn't told him anything. Alex and his dad didn't do the talking thing much.

She had to rethink her whole game plan quickly. "Yes?" Mrs. Manes asked. Her eyes were red and puffy, as if she'd been crying. "Oh, Isabel. I didn't recognize you for a second. I was—come on in."

"If it's no trouble," Isabel said. "I don't want to bother you—"

"No trouble at all," Mrs. Manes broke in. "Please. I could use the company."

Mrs. Manes led Isabel through the wide foyer into the casual yet tastefully decorated living room. She sat in a short leather upholstered armchair and faced Isabel. "So, what can I do for you?"

"I can't stop thinking about Alex," Isabel answered. Her voice squeaked a little as she said his name, but she steeled herself and plowed on. "I've been worried about him. I guess . . . I guess I just wanted to see how you've been holding up and if you've heard anything."

Mrs. Manes picked at the seam of the leather armchair for a long moment, and when she looked up at Isabel again, her eyes glistened with tears. Her mouth twitched as she tried to reply. "I'm . . . I'm sorry," she said finally. "It's just that, with you being so concerned, I suppose I was caught off guard." A tear rolled down her cheek, and she wiped it away. "I'm not usually like this," Mrs. Manes explained. "I've been trying to be strong—"

"You don't have to be strong," Isabel said softly. "Nobody's asking that of you."

"If only that were true," Mrs. Manes replied. She rearranged herself on the chair and cleared her throat. "Listen, I've got one son in the marines and two in the air force. I've worked hard at preparing myself for any eventuality, no matter how grim. But this is *Alex* we're talking about. Alex is different. He's—"

"Sweet," Isabel supplied.

"Sweet," Mrs. Manes agreed. "I know my youngest. He wouldn't have run away, not without leaving some sort of note. Which means something must have happened to him. . . ."

Mrs. Manes's face crumpled up, and the tears spilled over onto her pale cheeks.

Isabel knew she wasn't going to win any awards as the world's warmest person, but she had to do something. She stood up and walked over to Alex's mother and covered her hand with her own.

"Mrs. Manes," Isabel said. "You don't know what's happened. Nobody does. He could walk through that door any minute."

I wish, Isabel added silently.

"Thank you," Mrs. Manes said, clinging to Isabel's hand. Isabel almost cringed. The woman's fingers were so cold—as if the life were seeping out of her. "Thank you for your kind words. It means a lot to me."

"No problem," Isabel said. "Can I get you a cup of tea or something? Or maybe you should lie down for a while? You don't look like you've slept since . . . in ages."

"I could use a rest," Mrs. Manes said. "But my husband has the police calling in on the hour, and he calls even more frequently than that. I've got to answer those calls—"

"I'll handle it," Isabel offered. "You go lie down and take a good nap, and I'll cover for you for an hour or so. Okay?"

"You're an angel," Mrs. Manes said eagerly. "Now I know why my son thinks the world of you. But just for an hour or so. Promise you'll wake me then?"

Isabel nodded. "I'll just be here, watching TV," she said as Mrs. Manes rose from her chair and headed down the hall.

When Mrs. Manes had left the living room, Isabel did turn on the television, but she turned the volume down low so she could hear Alex's mother moving through the house. Isabel flipped around for a while, stopping on the shopping network, which had a special on metallic nail polishes. She watched that impatiently, waiting for Mrs. Manes to fall asleep.

When Isabel couldn't stand waiting another second, she got up from the couch and crept down

the hall, pausing outside Mrs. Manes's open bedroom door. Alex's mother's breathing was slow and
regular—perfect.

Isabel hurried as fast and as silently as she could
in the opposite direction. She had her destination
firmly in mind from what she remembered from
Alex's tour of the house.

Mr. Manes's office.

In the center of the room was a huge wooden
desk with a laptop computer. Isabel sat down in
the Major's leather chair and popped open the laptop, pushing the power switch. She found a half-
empty box of disks and began to copy as many files
as she could from a directory marked Private. As
she copied, Isabel listened for any sign of movement outside the office. The Maneses' house was as
silent as a tomb.

The whirring of the disk drive sounded awfully
loud to Isabel's ears. What could she say to explain
why she was using the computer if Mrs. Manes
found her in there? She was looking for the latest
version of *Doom*? I don't think so, Isabel thought.

If Mrs. Manes found her, Isabel would have to
knock her out and try to scramble her memory. As
distasteful as that idea was, she couldn't think of
any other way to escape.

When the Private files were copied onto disk,
Isabel clicked around for a few moments, looking
for anything else that seemed appropriate. She

passed up the Major's financial records and personal correspondence and left his Memos folder alone. Then, in a subdirectory marked Xtra, she found a folder titled *Tabula Rasa*.

Vaguely Isabel recalled something from some PBS philosophy show her mom had on one night while Isabel was doing her homework. Apparently some philosophers thought that human children were born without any instincts or memories—just an empty brain. And that empty brain, if Isabel remembered correctly, was called a *tabula rasa*.

The phrase was Latin. In English it roughly translated as "blank slate."

A chill ran up Isabel's arms and down her spine. Blank slate. Clean slate. Bingo, she thought.

She inserted a fresh disk and copied and pasted the folder into the A drive. Now that Isabel might have found something important, the drive seemed to be taking forever to copy. Hurry up, she ordered it. Can't you go any faster?

Then the phone rang.

Isabel thought she was going to jump out of her skin. But she forced herself to calm down as she picked up the office extension.

"Hello?" she said as cheerfully as she could manage. "The Maneses' residence."

"Who's this?" a gruff voice demanded. "Where's my wife?"

"This is Isabel," she replied politely, although

the bristling sound of the Major's voice set her teeth on edge. "I'm a friend of your son's. We met a few weeks ago? I'm answering the phone for Mrs. Manes while she rests."

"Oh," the Major said. "Thank you. Tell her I called when she gets up."

"Of course," Isabel said. "I certainly will." Being so polite made her teeth ache.

"Good." Mr. Manes coughed softly, and then he hung up without saying good-bye.

Isabel replaced the receiver and concentrated on listening, blood pounding in her temples. Had the phone call woken Mrs. Manes?

When she didn't hear anything for a few moments, Isabel sighed with relief and checked the computer's progress. The files were all copied. She pulled out the disk and added it to the two others she'd made.

Isabel checked her watch and quickly shut down the computer. Why did I tell her I'd stay? she thought nervously. She had to get out of here and bring these files to Max so he could sort through them. Part of her wanted to ditch, but she couldn't do that to Mrs. Manes. She could hang out and let the woman sleep—give Alex's mom a little comfort.

After everything Isabel had done to Alex, she figured she owed him that much.

Isabel burst into her family's kitchen and found Max sitting at the table. He was munching spicy tortilla chips and peanut butter, a snack they both loved. She waved the disks in front of him.

"Guess what I got?" she asked excitedly. It had taken forever for Mrs. Manes to get herself out of bed, and Isabel couldn't hold her news in any longer.

"Proof that aliens live among us?" Max guessed, dipping a chip.

"Such a comedic genius," Isabel said, rolling her eyes. "On these disks I happen to have copies of Mr. Manes's private files. And get this—one of the files is named *Tabula Rasa!*"

Max's eyes opened wide. "No way," he said. "Where did you get those?"

"Reconnaissance mission to the Maneses' house," Isabel informed him.

Max frowned. "Isabel," he said in the big-brother voice that drove her up the wall, "are you out of your mind? I thought we decided that we'd leave the Major alone—"

"Chill," Isabel told him. "I knew you'd start freaking, but I got in and out, no problem."

"Do you know how dangerous that could have been?" Max continued. "Michael or I should have come along . . . as backup, at least. What if you'd gotten caught?"

"But I wasn't," Isabel replied, tossing her long blond hair over her shoulder. "Now, do you want to lecture me all day, or do you want to go up to your laptop and see what's in these files?"

Max heaved a big sigh as he started out of the kitchen. "Let's go see what you've got."

"Wait," Isabel said. "Bring the chips."

Up in his room, Max took a seat at his desk, and Isabel hovered over his shoulder. "Forget the Personal disks," Isabel suggested. "Go right for *Tabula Rasa.*"

"Right," Max said, clicking around with his mouse. The folder contained several files, all named with numbers. But when Max clicked open file 1.mxl, the screen filled with nonsense characters. Pure gibberish.

"This program doesn't support this type of file," Max explained in frustration.

"Do you have a program that does?" Isabel asked.

"Maybe. I've got a translator that's pretty new." Max started the program, but it crashed the system, causing the little hourglass cursor to spin endlessly in the center of the screen.

As Max rebooted, Isabel ground her teeth. "What's the matter?"

"I think they're encrypted," Max said. "I'm not going to be able to open these files. Sorry, Iz. All that work for nothing."

"Encrypted," Isabel repeated. "If the Major's encrypting stuff, he's got to be hiding something, don't you think? He's got to be Clean Slate."

"We shouldn't jump to any conclusions," Max said.

But Isabel knew she was right. Encrypted files.

Tabula rasa. The photograph of Mr. Manes shaking hands with the thankfully deceased Sheriff Valenti.

It all pointed to one inescapable conclusion. Valenti might be dead, but now they had a new force to contend with.

And Mr. Manes was just a little too close to Isabel and her friends for comfort. Make that a lot too close.

The Crashdown Café was a madhouse.

Maria had been working her butt off all afternoon, and she still had another half hour before her break. She navigated her way through the aisle of the Ortechos' diner with a teeming tray on her arm, sidestepping a little girl who was running back to her table. At least tips will be good, Maria reminded herself as she served three out-of-towners at a window table. The tourists who came to Roswell to check out UFO central might be annoying, but they usually tipped decently.

As Maria headed across the room to take the order of a couple who had just sat down, she glanced across the restaurant. Adam and Michael were hanging out in a booth in Liz's area. Liz hurried by them, rushing to the pick-up window, and Maria smiled to herself as she watched Adam following Liz with his eyes.

The boy had it bad. Maria had felt the same expression cross her face too many times when she looked at Michael. She could recognize a major crush when she saw one. She just hoped it didn't look as sweetly pathetic on her. But of course it probably did.

Michael, Maria thought as she half listened to the new couple's drink order. My good friend Michael.

"I'd like an iced tea, no sugar," the woman said.

Maria nodded absently. It wasn't easy slipping back into thinking of Michael as just a friend. Understatement. It was one of the most painful processes of her entire life.

But that's the way Michael wanted it, so that's the way it would be.

Friends.

Good friends.

One of her best friends.

"Miss, are you even listening to me?" the man at the table in front of her asked.

"Oh," Maria said. "Oh, sure. You wanted an ice-cream sundae, right? With a cherry?"

"No," the man said. "I wanted a beer."

"Right," Maria replied. "Beer."

As she bustled away to get the drinks, Maria caught a cute girl shooting Michael a flirty look. Please, just don't let him start bringing some girl around me, she thought. At least not for a while. Not until I've . . . mended a little more.

Maria filled a plastic tumbler with iced tea. When he does find some girl, some girl he looks at the way he looks at Cameron, Maria told herself sternly, you are not going to allow yourself to be pulverized again. You will still be Michael's buddy. Get used to the idea of him dating because it's going to happen.

She put the iced tea on a tray, along with a bottle of beer and a tall glass. Maybe we'll even discuss what to get Michael's girlfriend for Valentine's Day and stuff, Maria thought, like I do with Alex.

Why don't I just stick needles in my eyes while I'm at it?

As she brought the tray over to the tourist couple, Maria continued her conversation inside her head. Not pins, but needles, she clarified to herself. Because needles have nothing to stop them from traveling through your bloodstream until they pierce your heart.

Maria put the tourist woman's iced tea down too hard on the table, splashing some on the woman's T-shirt.

"Yikes, sorry," Maria said. "Here." She pulled a handful of napkins out of her apron and handed them to the shocked woman. "The tea's on the house."

Then Maria noticed the woman's T-shirt. Or rather, what was printed on it.

It was a logo for *My Favorite Martian,* the old TV show.

As Maria gave the guy his beer, she glanced at his T-shirt, too. Tourist couples often had matching or similar slogans on their shirts, which always amused Maria.

But his didn't match. Instead it proclaimed, I've Gone Underground . . . in Carlsbad Caverns! over a picture of the gigantic cave's yawning mouth.

Carlsbad Caverns, Maria thought, staring at his T-shirt. Could—

"Miss, is there something wrong?" the man asked.

"Uh, no," Maria replied. "Sorry, I was just spacing out. Are you ready to order your food?"

"Ten minutes ago," the woman piped up.

But Maria barely heard her.

Carlsbad Caverns. Stalactites? Check. Stalagmites? Check. Bats? Check. A possible hideout or whatever for DuPris, down deep in the cavern where no tourists or explorers ever went?

Check.

"Miss?" the man at her table asked. "Can we just forget about the food and get a check for the beer? *Quickly?*"

Check.

SEVEN

Liz grabbed the dashboard for support as Max drove over a pothole and her knee slammed into the center console. "That was pleasant," she grumbled, trying in vain to get comfortable. "We have to get ourselves a bigger car."

She was mashed in the shotgun seat of Max's Jeep with Maria, and she felt like her legs were going to be eternally cramped. Max was driving—somehow managing to hit every bump—and Adam, Isabel, and Michael were in the backseat.

Just be thankful that Papa let you come on this trip at all, Liz told herself. She loved her father, but the strain of constantly proving herself stable, responsible, completely Liz-not-Rosa was almost too much sometimes. She was hoping that the fact that he'd approved this weekend trip to Carlsbad Caverns meant he had actually developed some kind of trust in her.

Of course, Liz thought with a pang of guilt, he thinks Maria's mother is coming along with us. But still.

It hadn't hurt that Carlsbad Caverns was less

than a hundred miles from Roswell. It was a major tourist destination and a favorite campsite for lots of families in town. The grounds around and above the vast network of caves were a national park, and her father had been relieved to hear that the park was policed by rangers. Liz had known to come to that discussion armed with ammunition in the form of information off the Internet.

"I am so psyched for this trip!" Maria called out suddenly, turning to grin right in Liz's face. "I haven't been camping since forever."

"This is not a pleasure trip," Isabel said grumpily. "We're going there to find the guy who killed our parents."

"And hopefully find a way to get Alex back," Max added.

For a long moment they were all silent, all thinking about Alex.

"Still," Michael finally said, "I brought marshmallows."

Everyone cracked up, including Isabel, releasing the heavy tension. Liz caught Max's eye and smiled. Marshmallows, campfire, dark starry sky. It could be a pretty romantic night. If Max could stay focused on her long enough to enjoy it with her.

Liz glanced in the rearview mirror to see if Adam was staring at her. She had that hot back-of-the-neck feeling that made her think he was. Just as Max changed lanes, she caught sight of a small blue clunker a few cars back abruptly swerving to follow them. Liz's heart gave a hard double thump.

She craned her neck to look out the back, but Adam was blocking her view. And yes, he was staring. "Duck for a sec," Liz told him.

Sure enough, a blue Nissan Sentra was keeping pace with the Jeep. "Speed up a little," Liz said to Max. "I want to see something."

"Your wish is my command," Max said.

"Oh, please," Isabel said with obvious disgust.

Liz ignored her. "Maybe pass somebody, too," she suggested.

Michael sat up straight. "Is somebody following us?" he asked.

"That's what I'm trying to figure out," Liz replied.

Max accelerated, and the blue Nissan sped up, too. And as Max passed a slow truck in the right lane, the Nissan zoomed closer.

Liz's stomach dropped. "Oh yeah. We're being followed," she declared. "What do we do?"

"Is it the Major?" Isabel asked.

"I don't know. Can you see from back there?" Liz asked. "I can't make him out. Slow down a little, Max."

Max pressed his lips together and did as she asked. Caught off guard by Max's sudden deceleration, the Nissan caught up to the Jeep. And Liz could see that it wasn't Mr. Manes at the wheel.

It was Kyle Valenti.

"What does he want?" Isabel muttered, tension putting a sharp edge on her voice.

"After the way he freaked out on me, who knows?" Liz replied. "I told him I didn't know anything about his father, but he didn't come close to believing me."

"Like he would have believed the truth," Michael put in. "'Yeah, I know what happened. An evil alien turned your dad into a one-man Hiroshima'?"

"You're right," Liz agreed.

"He saw us!" Adam called out. "I mean, he saw us seeing him." Adam cleared his throat. "He knows he's been spotted."

Liz kept her eyes locked on the rearview mirror. Kyle accelerated until the Nissan was practically kissing the Jeep's bumper. His eyebrows knitted together, and his eyes grew squinty.

"Ohmigod!" Isabel cried. Her startled shout was still lingering in the air when Kyle rammed them from behind. The crunch of metal and the screeching of tires rang out as Max fought to keep the Jeep steady.

"Is he crazy?" Max shouted.

"Very possibly," Liz shot back, her heart going into high gear. She braced both hands against the dashboard.

Kyle bumped the Jeep again, shoving them to the left. He was playing for keeps, trying to force them into oncoming traffic.

"Do something!" Maria screamed. "Can't you blow out his tire?"

"I think he's close enough for us to aim, even though we're going so fast," Adam answered.

"Let's try it before he turns us into roadkill," Michael yelled, grabbing hands with Adam and Isabel.

A second later Liz heard a sharp report, like a gunshot, echo behind the Jeep. Liz watched through the rearview as Kyle's car started wobbling and then went careening off the highway into the shrubs and cacti of the desert. In moments they'd left him far behind.

"Good work," Max said.

"My friends, the superheroes," Maria added proudly.

"Do you think he had any idea where we were headed?" Michael asked, still staring out the back window.

"I didn't tell him," Liz replied, "although he could pretty easily find out by asking my father, if he thought of it."

"I wouldn't worry about it," Max said. "The park is huge. He'll never find us in there."

"Yeah, he's history," Isabel said.

Liz hoped Isabel was right. But Kyle could be persistent. And if Sheriff Valenti had told him anything about alien powers, a blown-out tire wouldn't make him give up.

It would just make him more suspicious.

"Hey, Max," Adam said, pulling a small gray laptop out from under his feet. "Why did you bring your computer?"

"I thought I might work at decoding some of those files Isabel found at the Major's," Max answered. "I don't think I'm gonna have much luck, though. I don't have the right software. And I don't think it's anything we can pick up at The Wiz."

Adam flipped open the screen and hit the power button. The computer whirred to life. "You don't need software," he said. "I used to do this all the time at the compound."

He opened up one of the files, and it flashed onto the screen—a jumbled mass of gibberish.

"Wait a minute," Michael said, shifting in his tight seat. "What do you mean, you don't need software?"

Adam smiled. "You guys are going to love this," he said. He loved it when he could show his friends a new power. At least then he didn't feel like the world's biggest two-year-old, asking stuff like, "What's Elvis?"

"It's like that Magic Eye book Ray had in the living room," he explained. "All you have to do is stare at the code for a while and eventually your brain sorts through the garbage and you can read the file."

"Seriously?" Isabel asked. "It's that simple?"

Adam shrugged. "Well, it takes some concentration, but it's not that hard."

"Cool. We have a secret weapon," Maria joked.

Taking a deep breath, Adam gazed at the screen. You can do this, he thought. Sheriff Valenti hadn't exactly been a candidate for Father of the Year. But

Valenti *had* been good at teaching Adam how to use his powers in many different, useful ways, even if most of those ways were violent. Adam had always been told that those practice exercises were "games," when actually Valenti was training him to be a living weapon or experimenting on him like a lab rat.

What a difference it was to use his powers to help his friends instead of to destroy Valenti's enemies.

For the next ten minutes Adam stared at the screen. His eyes started to burn, and a little pinprick of pain started digging into the back of his neck. But nothing was coming together. No pattern emerged. Frustrated, Adam closed the file and opened another in the folder.

"Tough going?" Michael asked.

"It's like the most complex code or cipher I've ever seen . . . times ten," Adam explained.

"Well, keep at it," Michael said. "You're the only one of us who can even begin to make sense out of that garbage."

Adam nodded, hoping Michael couldn't see how much what he'd just said meant to Adam. He concentrated on the new file and felt a little jolt as the symbols in front of him seemed to separate into distinct layers. The first four layers were just screens to confuse anyone who got their hands on this file, but the fifth layer . . .

The fifth layer had words.

As Adam read, his stomach turned over in

revulsion. He couldn't believe that there were people on this planet who would do such a thing . . . *plan* such a thing. The very idea of what he was reading made him want to cry, scream, tear out his hair—and fight back.

When he had finished, Adam sat for a moment, absorbing the magnitude of the horror he'd just read. How was he supposed to tell his friends?

"Um . . . you guys?" Adam called out, interrupting various conversations floating around the Jeep. "I managed to decode one of the files."

Instantly he had everyone's attention. The way Liz's eyes focused on him made Adam swallow with nervousness, so he turned to look at Michael.

"It's plans for a weapon," Adam said. "A chemical weapon."

"What does it do?" Maria asked.

Adam closed his eyes.

"It recognizes alien life-forms—and destroys them."

Maria's heart was slamming against her rib cage as she dug in her woven purse for her vial of cedar oil. She knew it would calm her down, and she'd never needed calming more badly than she did at that moment.

"A chemical weapon?" Isabel said faintly.

"It looks like all they have to do is release this gas into the air and it takes effect immediately," Adam said slowly. "But only on extraterrestrial cells."

114

"What is wrong with these people?" Isabel asked. "Why do they hate us so much?"

Maria found the bottle she was looking for, unscrewed the cap, and inhaled. She tried to picture herself walking through a forest of the ancient trees, but all she could see was people she loved lying dead on the ground.

"Houston, we have a problem," Michael announced. "Another one."

Maria followed his gaze and caught a glimpse of flashing lights. Red and blue lights. A police cruiser was approaching up the highway. With a gasp Maria spilled the entire contents of the vial into her lap.

"Max, you'd better pull over," Liz said.

"Can't we just blow out the police car's tires, too?" Adam asked.

"Not a good idea," Michael answered. "They could just radio ahead and get someone else to stop us."

"Maria, can't you do something about that smell?" Isabel asked. "It's gagging me."

"We're in a Jeep. Deal," Maria snapped as Max slowed down and drove onto the shoulder.

The cruiser pulled up behind them, and Maria was stunned to see Sheriff Dodson climb out of the police car and stride up the road, carrying a lumpy, rolled package.

Is she Clean Slate? Maria thought frantically. Is that one of the Major's chemical weapons she's carrying?

"This is all we need," Isabel whispered.

The sheriff stopped next to Maria and nailed her with a cool glance that made Maria want to confess everything, even stuff she hadn't done. "Hi," Maria said in a rush. "I know we're not supposed to ride with two of us in the front seat like this, but the Jeep was the best car to take camping, and—"

"No, you're not supposed to ride like that," Sheriff Dodson said. "But that's not why I'm here." Then she handed Maria the package she was carrying. Maria just stared at it in her hands, unable to recognize it for a moment.

"It's your sleeping bag," the sheriff said. "You forgot it, and I told your mom I'd track you down and give it to you."

"Oh, thanks," Maria said. She wondered if she sounded as dumbfounded as she felt.

Then Sheriff Dodson got a whiff of the cedar oil. "That's some interesting perfume you're wearing, Maria."

Maria giggled uncontrollably. A voice in the back of her mind told her she was acting like a freak, but she was too nervous to stop. "It's cedar oil," she exclaimed through her laughter. "It was an accident! I'm going to smell like this all day! Maybe even for the rest of my life."

Shut up, she ordered herself. Please, please, just shut up and let Sheriff Dodson go.

"Are you okay?" Sheriff Dodson asked, peering through the window at the rest of Maria's friends. Maria's heart pounded. The sheriff was probably thinking her bizarre behavior was drug induced or something.

She took a deep breath. "I'm fine," she said. "I just feel like an idiot. . . . You know, making you come out here with my bag and spilling oil all over me." She paused and looked into the sheriff's amused face. Maria blushed. "Sorry."

"That's okay," Sheriff Dodson said. She patted the side of the Jeep. "You kids have fun." Then with a small wave she turned and headed back to her cruiser.

Maria pressed her hands to her forehead and groaned.

"I feel like I just swallowed a pair of spiked heels," Isabel said.

"That was pretty intense," Max agreed. He waited for Sheriff Dodson's car to pass them before he headed back out onto the road.

"Maria," Michael said, "I'd suggest you start checking that sleeping bag for some sort of tracking device."

Maria giggled, clutching the bag to her chest.

Michael just looked at her. "I'm not kidding."

It was dark by the time Max had found a place to park and everybody had agreed on where to set up camp. Max liked the spot they'd chosen. It was a mile or so from the main cavern in an area called Whites City, out in the backcountry open desert but protected from the wind by a jagged, crumbling outcropping of dark red rock. Nearby, large serrated cacti cast eerie shadows in the moonlight.

"So, we'll just camp out tonight and then take the first tour of the caverns in the morning?" Maria asked, dropping her bag on the ground.

"Yeah," Max said. "I think we should get a sense of the place first."

"How are we going to know if DuPris is there?" Liz asked, pulling the cooler out of the Jeep. "It's not like the guide's going to point him out along with the bats and other interesting features."

"Well, with luck he'll use his powers and we'll be able to sense him," Michael said. He pulled on his jacket and handed Max his sweater.

"We're probably going to have to go into the closed-off section," Max said. "Hope everyone's ready for some spelunking."

"Some what?" Adam asked.

"He's just trying to sound like he knows what he's talking about," Isabel said. "Ignore him."

"Cave exploring," Michael explained. He shook his head. "I can't believe I actually associate with someone who uses the word *spelunking* in conversation." He turned to Adam. "I'm going to make a fire. Help me out?"

"Sure," Adam said. "What do I do?"

Max smiled. Sometimes Adam was like a puppy dog around Michael. And the amazing part was that Michael actually put up with it.

"Go out and collect some dried tumble-weeds—thick ones if you can find them," Michael instructed.

Soon the fire was roaring, sending up sparks and smoke into the starlit sky. Everyone gathered around the fire, pulling out food they'd brought.

"Guys? What are we going to do if we don't find DuPris?" Maria asked tentatively as she settled to the ground. "I mean, without the Stone . . ." She trailed off, leaving only the crackling of the fire to break the tense silence.

"Without the Stone, how are we going to bring Alex back," Max finished finally.

"We're gonna find him," Isabel said firmly, staring into the fire. "I know we are."

"And that's the attitude we should keep," Max said, looking at each of his friends. "We're going to find DuPris, and we're going to figure out a way to bring Alex home safely. We have to believe it, or we shouldn't even bother trying."

Liz looked up at him and smiled. "Right," she said firmly. "Tomorrow we bring Alex back."

"Right," Maria repeated.

Michael slapped his hands together. "Well, now that we're all settled on that, let's eat."

"Mr. Sensitive," Isabel muttered.

"What?" Michael asked, his eyes wide. "Alex wouldn't want us to starve."

Liz laughed. "The man has a point. Alex did—"

She corrected herself quickly. "Does. Alex does love his food."

"And so do I," Michael answered. He reached out and grabbed the Tupperware container filled with nachos from the café. "Mine," he said, cradling the nachos close to his chest and stroking the blue plastic lid lovingly. "Mine."

Max ripped open a bag of Cosmic Crunch, stuffed a handful into his mouth, and passed the bag to Liz. It's like a celebration before the apocalypse, he thought, feeling a little creeped out. Enjoy yourself now because tomorrow . . . who knows what will happen?

"Max? I brought jalapeño potato chips and soy sauce just for you," Liz said, holding up a bright red bag.

"Thanks," Max said with a small smile. "But I think I'll go for a walk first."

Liz's lips tightened slightly, and Max's heart responded with a sharp pang. "I'll be right back," he promised. Then he shoved himself to his feet and headed off before she could argue or volunteer to come with him.

Max found a big shrub a few yards from the campsite and took a seat on a large flat rock behind it. He needed to connect to the consciousness.

Connect more deeply, to be exact. The connection was never broken anymore.

Max concentrated on shutting out the sounds

of his friends and took a deep breath. He hadn't told the others about his encounter with Alex. He didn't want to worry them, and he'd been hoping against hope that the anger had died down. That Alex wasn't so terrified.

"Just let me be right," Max muttered.

He leaned back and opened himself up to the maelstrom of images hovering at the back of his mind. Then he waited for the sense of belonging that always greeted him on his immersion into the consciousness.

Instead he was enveloped in a pocket of rage. Shrieks of fury in frenzied voices swirled around him from beings surrounding him. Max felt like he'd been sucked into a whirlpool of lava and then tossed to crash against jagged, molten rocks.

These beings were calling for Alex's life to be extinguished. They wanted him dead.

Now.

EIGHT

Isabel leaned against Michael's shoulder, enjoying the flickering warmth of the bonfire. Michael felt solid against her arm. Comforting and protective.

Brotherly.

"How was it I ever thought I could date you?" she asked Michael cheerfully, tilting her head back to look up at him. "It would have been a huge mistake."

"Definitely. But you're beautiful and I'm beautiful, so it seemed to make sense at the time," Michael joked.

Isabel sat up on the thick plastic pad she'd brought with her. "Beautiful! Beautiful? You're so conceited!" she squealed.

"Men are not beautiful," Maria jumped in. "Only women can be beautiful."

"I am beautiful, and you both know it," Michael replied with a smile.

"God!" Isabel exclaimed. "You're more arrogant than I am."

"Nah, it's not arrogance," Michael said. "It's just a basic understanding of reality."

"See?" Isabel said to the others. "Total arrogance."

"He's self-centered, too," Maria piped up.

Isabel grinned. Maria deserved to get in a few jabs of her own.

"Hey!" Michael protested. "Don't hate me because I'm beautiful, all right?"

"We don't," Maria reassured him. Then she gave him a long look up and down. "In fact, I've changed my mind. I do think you're beautiful."

"Hey!" Isabel protested.

"Thank you," Michael said primly.

"And you're lucky you are," Maria continued. She leaned closer to him. "Because if you weren't beautiful, we'd have no use for you. You're way too conceited!"

"Go, Maria," Isabel said, impressed. Who knew the girl had it in her?

Michael rolled his eyes and pretended to ignore them.

"Michael, Michael," Isabel continued, enjoying herself. "So vain, it's insane."

"I am not listening to this," Michael said.

"That rhymes," Maria called. "It's a song."

Isabel laughed, watching Michael's face start to turn red. "Michael, Michael," she repeated, adding a lilt to her voice. "So conceited . . . I'm defeated."

"That doesn't even make sense," Michael protested, obviously trying hard to keep his cool.

"Yes, it does," Adam jumped in.

"Michael, Michael," Maria sang. "So arrogant, he makes the girls pant."

"All right, that's it," Michael said. He grabbed

124

the bag of marshmallows away from Adam. "One more little rhyme from either of you and it's war."

Right, Isabel thought. I'm so scared.

"Michael, Michael," she sang, batting her eyelashes at him. "So egotistical, it's almost . . . metaphysical."

Michael flung a marshmallow, and she felt it bop onto her forehead. He instantly doubled over in laughter.

Isabel narrowed her eyes at him. "You're so dead." While he was busy laughing, she grabbed the bag of marshmallows out of his grasp and pulled one out.

"Don't even think about it," Michael said. He had stopped laughing.

"Oh, you have no idea what I'm thinking, my friend," Isabel said. She hurled the marshmallow at Michael. It flew off into the desert, missing him by at least five feet. Isabel winced. Her aim had never been that great. Michael shook his head, laughing at her lack of coordination.

Irritated, Isabel reached out and *snapped* the marshmallow with her mind. It had already passed Michael by, but it veered awkwardly and hit him on the back of the head.

"My turn!" Maria shouted. She tore open a second bag and began lobbing marshmallows in Michael's direction.

Michael picked up marshmallows that had landed near him and returned fire at both Maria and Isabel. Liz screeched and scrambled away from the fray while Adam just looked on with interest.

As Isabel ducked and threw, she decided that Liz and Adam shouldn't be allowed to stay neutral in this war. Her next volley was directed at their heads.

Suddenly they had a full-fledged marshmallow fight on their hands. Shrieks of laughter filled the night sky.

My friends are *so* juvenile, Isabel thought, whipping another marshmallow into the fray.

Liz mashed a marshmallow on Adam's forehead, then turned to flee. But before she could make a move, Adam grabbed her around the waist, wielding two marshmallows with his free hand.

Liz screamed but was silenced when Adam stuffed the two marshmallows into her mouth. She started to laugh, but when she sucked in her breath, she pulled her mouthful of marshmallow goo down into her throat. In a moment of panic she realized the goo had lodged there. She wasn't getting any air.

As she gasped for breath, Liz saw Adam's eyes widen in horrified shock. He pounded on her back as Liz attempted to force the marshmallows either up or down.

I just want to breathe, her brain screamed as her eyes watered. Breathe!

Finally she swallowed painfully and took a gulp of air. She dissolved into coughs, and Adam stopped pounding and started rubbing her back soothingly.

His hands were warm and comforting as she dropped shakily to the ground, holding her aching throat with both hands. Adam sat with her.

"Sorry! I'm so sorry! Are you okay?" he asked. His hands were still touching her back, lightly caressing her shoulder blades.

All Liz's perceptions focused on the touch of Adam's hand. She felt light-headed, almost as if she were tipsy. "Who spiked the 'mallows?" she mumbled.

I felt like this when we were dancing, Liz remembered, her thoughts coming slow and somehow soft. It felt . . . good.

Liz frowned. When had they gone dancing? Suddenly the dream she'd had the other night flooded back to her. Adam was there. He had done something to a nightmare she'd been having. He'd changed it, made it safe.

"You were in my dream."

"Liz, I'm so sorry," Adam said gently, his breath against her ear. His low voice sent a tingling shiver down her side. "I wasn't trying to spy on you or anything. I just—"

"Don't worry about it." Liz jumped up. "I'm going to bring Max some marshmallows," she blurted out. She grabbed an almost empty package off the ground. "He loves these things."

Liz ran her hand through her hair as she walked away from the campfire. She suddenly realized she was trembling, and she wrapped her arms around herself. Things had been getting a little . . . *complicated* there with Adam for a moment.

She had to see Max. Right now.

Where had he disappeared to, anyway? When he wandered away from the campfire, Liz had assumed he wanted to find someplace private to connect with the collective consciousness, but he'd been gone a long time. Too long.

Liz shook her head. She was actually feeling jealous of a group of beings on a planet that was so far away, it couldn't be seen from the earth. She was losing it.

She kept walking, trying to enjoy the peace of the desert and not get all crazed. Her feet crunched on the dry ground as she wandered in a rough circle around the campsite.

She was about to give it up—or start screaming his name like a loon—when she spotted him. He was sitting cross-legged on a rock, staring away from her. His skin seemed to glow with a slight silver tint in the starlight.

Liz hurried over to him. "Hey, Max—"

She froze when she got a good look at his face. His eyes were glazed, expressionless, and his cheeks were slack. There was more movement in the vast emptiness of the desert than in Max Evans's body. He looked like the living embodiment of a black hole.

Liz shivered. She knew Max was just connected

to the consciousness, but the sight of him so motionless and . . . *vacant* was deeply disturbing.

For a second she considered shaking him. But Max would only be annoyed that she'd interrupted him—not the mood she wanted him in. She turned away and began walking slowly toward the camp.

Why couldn't she have found Max talking to a cute girl or something? At least Liz knew how to deal with other girls.

When she reached the campfire, Liz hesitated. Maybe this wasn't the best plan. Adam was over there, and . . . Well, it just wasn't a good idea.

I should just pack it in, Liz thought as she veered off to the flat area where they'd all set up their sleeping bags. Tomorrow's going to be a long day, anyway.

As she crawled into her sleeping bag, Liz pushed aside a strong feeling of disappointment. This wasn't the way she'd expected to be going to sleep when she'd first heard about this trip. She'd been looking forward to falling asleep curled up beside Max after some romance under the stars. Obviously that wasn't going to happen.

Liz closed her eyes and sighed, willing herself to stop obsessing and go to sleep.

But right before she drifted off, a thought crept into her mind unbidden, causing her heart to skip a beat.

Would Adam visit her in her dream again?

* * *

Even though the night had become cool, Michael's face felt hot and sweaty. The marshmallow war had been good exercise. He began to pick up the dirty marshmallows off the ground, tossing them into the fire.

"We didn't save any to roast," he complained. "All day I'd been looking forward to toasting marshmallows on a stick, and now we wasted them all."

"It wasn't a waste," Isabel said with a smile at Maria. "At least we managed to kick the guys' butts."

"Keep dreaming," Michael said. "You two were running for cover. Adam and I dominated, right?" He looked at Adam expectantly.

"Right," Adam said, sounding less than enthused.

Michael felt for the guy. Liz had taken off kind of abruptly, and it was obvious Adam had a crush on her. It wasn't that Michael wanted Max and Liz to break up. Max was his best friend, and Michael thought Max and Liz made a good couple. But Michael knew what it felt like to get your heart trampled on.

But Michael was *not* going to think about Cameron.

"Oh, please," Maria said. "Isabel and I beat you and Adam into the ground with our patented marshmallow bombardment."

"Guys don't know how to fight," Isabel added. "Oh, they think they're so tough, with their wars and everything, but for true combat, we girls win every time. Just think of that old saying, 'Hell hath no fury—'"

"Get real," Michael interrupted. "If *Alex* was here, we would have . . ."

Michael let his words trail off. Mentioning Alex had been a mistake. The party had crashed with a thud almost loud enough for Michael to hear. Everybody stared into the embers of the fire.

"Hey," Michael said, trying to salvage the evening, "you know those lists Alex used to make?"

"Like the one about bad business ideas," Maria said. "That was one of my favorites."

"Exactly," Michael said. "So I was thinking—"

"What was the number-one idea?" Isabel asked.

"Months-of-the-year underpants," Maria replied. "Alex is so twisted."

"Hello!" Michael shouted, and his friends turned to look at him. "As I was saying, Alex's web site has been just sitting there since he got transported. And it's getting old fast. So we could—"

"Update it!" Maria filled in. "So it's like we haven't forgotten about him. He'd be kind of still here."

"Great idea," Michael said sarcastically. "Why didn't I think of that?"

"I've got the laptop," Adam said. He pulled out Max's computer from his knapsack.

"We can't upload anything since we don't have a phone, but we can make the list and then put it on-line later," Isabel said.

Maria clapped and then rubbed her hands together. "Okay, let's go. Who's got an idea for a list?"

"Favorite kinds of toast?" Adam offered. "There's wheat, and rye, and with jam—"

"No," Isabel said. "Next."

"Um . . . ," Maria began. "How about 'The Ten Best Holidays'? We could pick little ones, like Groundhog's Day or Flag Day."

"Nah," Michael decided. "Needs more of an edge. How about 'The Five Coolest Foreign Cars'?"

"And that has an *edge*?" Maria asked, crossing her arms over her chest.

"They're *foreign* cars," Michael explained.

"Lame," Isabel said. "Let's do 'The Ten Ways to a Man's Heart.' That's perfect."

"Perfect?" Maria asked. "For Alex? His father and his brothers would kill him. Alex is sensitive, but he's not *that* sensitive."

"I withdraw the suggestion," Isabel said.

Everyone fell silent, once again staring into the fire. This is hard, Michael thought. No wonder Alex was always rewriting his lists.

"No other ideas?" Maria asked.

Nobody replied.

Isabel heaved a giant sigh. "I think we should just give up," she said. "Trying to think like Alex is just making me miss him more."

Michael nodded. Thinking like Alex was impossible.

Because Alex was the only Alex.

NINE

Adam took a deep breath of the dank air of Carlsbad Caverns and smiled. Somehow the dark caves felt like home.

Which was actually pretty sick. Sick, but true.

As planned, Adam and the others were on the first morning tour. They'd avoided the Red Tour, which took the elevator down into the caves, and opted for the Blue Tour. This one followed a winding switchback trail down from the enormous cave mouth to the famous Big Room. Adam's group was bringing up the rear of the tour just in case they had to veer off the beaten path undetected.

They'd already passed the thousand-year-old Native American paintings near the entrance and had walked along a black asphalt paved path through several smaller rooms with fantastic limestone formations. In his head Adam ran through the names of some of the most spectacular natural creations: the Iceberg Rock, the Veiled Statue in the Green Lake Room, the Soda Straw formations in the Papoose Room, the ornate natural rock sculptures in the King's Palace.

He hurried to keep up with the tour group as

they passed the six-story-high formations in the Hall of Giants, heading toward the Big Room.

Suddenly Adam stopped short. He'd felt something . . . a little tingle, like someone had run a feather down his spine.

Somebody nearby was using power. Power no human possessed.

The twinge hadn't been enough for Adam to be able to locate the source, but it was close. In the cavern.

Adam rushed over to his friends and grabbed Michael's shoulder.

"I think DuPris is nearby," Adam whispered hoarsely.

Michael's eyes grew sharp. "Where?" he asked. "How do you know?"

"Didn't you feel it?" Adam asked. "He was using his powers."

"Shhh! Not so loud," Max said. He led Michael and Adam over to a fat, rippled stalagmite, away from the rest of the tour group. Liz, Maria, and Isabel followed. "Now, what did you feel?"

"Just a little tingle," Adam replied. "Somebody using their power, but I couldn't tell where it was coming from. Neither of you felt it?" he asked, searching their faces.

"I didn't," Michael answered. "But your powers are more developed than ours."

They needed him. That realization still gave him a rush.

"Let's keep looking around," Max said decisively. "We'll rejoin the tour. Everyone just act normal. Adam, tell us right away if you feel it again, okay?"

"I will," Adam promised.

Adam hung out beside Liz as the group moved into the Big Room—the second-largest cave room in the world. The tour group guide said that the largest cave was in Borneo.

Adam stared up at the high, pointy ceiling of the vast cave. The room was so big, it wouldn't even have felt like it was underground . . . if it wasn't so dark. The people who ran the park had done a good job with placing small lights around the room. Adam couldn't see any of the fixtures, but the more stunning formations were backlit, illuminating their eerie shapes and colors and throwing mysterious shadows on the cave walls.

Although for some reason he found that his eyes kept drifting away from the awesome sight over to Liz. Another awesome sight.

As the park ranger led them around the edge of the Big Room to a small, damp offshoot called the Painted Grotto, Adam felt another twinge of power and stopped.

Liz turned around, her brow creased with concern. "Do you feel it again?"

Adam opened his mouth to answer, but before he could, a blast of sizzling, white-hot power slammed into his heart and vibrated through every molecule of his body. Adam strained against the overpowering pain, closing his eyes to keep them from bursting out of their sockets. The pain was viciously intense, and Adam was vaguely aware that he was shaking violently.

Make it stop, he begged silently. Someone make it stop.

And then it did.

Adam gasped in a ragged breath. His eyes felt dry and shriveled, but he managed to blink and look around. Max was pressing his hand to his chest hard, and Isabel was grasping Max's arm, her eyes closed. Michael's fists were clenched, and he stared at Adam, his eyes wide.

"What happened?" Maria asked, her voice trembling.

"You felt that one," Adam said.

"Oh yeah," Michael agreed in a low voice.

"If I never have that experience again in my life, it'll be too soon," Isabel said, still clinging to her brother. "What *was* that?"

"DuPris," Adam answered. "At least I think so. It sure felt like the Stone of Midnight to me. What else is that powerful? And it was pretty close this time."

Liz slipped her hand into Max's and looked into his eyes, brushing a lock of hair from his forehead.

"Are you okay?" she asked in a low, caring voice.

The pang to Adam's heart was almost as painful as the shock had been.

"We're losing the tour group," Adam said flatly. "Should we catch up?"

"No," Max said. "I think we're close to finding

what we came here for. Could anyone tell where the power was coming from?"

Adam closed his eyes, blocking out the sight of Liz's concerned expression, and forced himself to remember the shock . . . to feel it again so that he could concentrate on which direction it had come from.

"That way," he said, pointing toward a path that led away from the Big Room. It was a walkway with a steep slope—so steep that the asphalt paved over it was made with textured ridges in it to help with traction. "It's down there."

"Let's go," Michael said, his tone grim.

Adam started down the path, his friends following close behind as they picked their way down the damp, slippery route. He braced himself for another sudden shock of stinging energy, but it never came.

Adam felt comfortable leading the group. He ducked under a low, misshapen overhang and skirted a stone "drapery" that ran down a wall, the rock patterned like hanging curtains. Then he came face-to-face with a swinging chain cordoning off a tunnel that led into darkness. The paved path ended there.

"What do we do?" Adam asked.

"We keep going," Max said. "We can't stop now."

Adam nodded. He swung his leg over the chain.

"Hey!" a deep voice shouted from up the corridor. "You can't go in there."

Adam yanked his leg back onto the asphalt

path. A young ranger, dressed in his uniform of a brown shirt and green trousers, was hurrying toward them. His almost childlike features wore a stern expression.

Isabel stepped up to face the ranger, smiling flirtatiously and looking up at him with her big, blue eyes. "We're sorry," she said. "We didn't realize we weren't allowed in there. We'll stay on the path from now on."

"See that you do," the ranger said with less certainty. "It's dangerous in the back tunnels, and leaving the path is a felony."

"A felony?" Maria squeaked.

"These caves are a World Heritage Site and a natural preserve, miss," the ranger answered. "Foot traffic destroys them."

"No problem. We're not looking for trouble," Michael said, shooting Adam an ironic smile. Michael turned and started back up the slope.

Adam reluctantly followed the group back to the Big Room. They'd been so close. Why did that ranger guy have to wander along at that moment? But at least now they had reason to hope. They knew where DuPris was hiding.

And felony or no, Adam knew that his friends weren't about to give up that easily.

"Is it time yet?" Maria asked. She knew that she'd asked that question a dozen times in the last hour, but anticipating the showdown with DuPris was driving her crazy. Plus she was out of cedar oil to calm herself down.

Max glanced at his watch. "Yeah, we should be okay now," he said. "The last tour ended an hour and a half ago."

Maria nodded and tapped her foot nervously, staring out at the vastness of the desert.

She and her friends were standing a hundred or so yards from the cavern parking lot, behind a low mesa. It had taken them a few hours to walk out from the caves to this spot, but they wouldn't have to walk back. Not when they had Max around.

"Everyone ready?" Max asked.

Maria took a deep breath and reached out to grab Liz's hand. Adam took Maria's other hand, and Maria glanced across the circle at Michael. Part of Maria wanted to be holding hands with him, but that wouldn't do anything good for her resolve to be just friends. Touching him and still thinking of Michael as a friend was impossible.

"You okay with this?" Michael asked Max. "You've only moved us this way once before—"

"And you're still kind of weak," Liz pointed out.

"I can do it," Max said. His voice was so firm and sure that a tense knot of fear in Maria's shoulders loosened. She hadn't even realized how rigid she'd been holding them until the stiffness disappeared.

Michael nodded once, and then he grabbed Max's hand, completing the circle. The force of the connection surged through Maria, and she welcomed the comforting warmth that came with it.

Their auras—Max's emerald green, Michael's brick red, Maria's own sparkling blue, Liz's warm amber, Isabel's rich purple, and Adam's bright yellow—blended into one potent rainbow.

Maria wasn't sure what to call Max's bizarre method of transportation. She'd heard DuPris mention something called a *lavila*, which she'd assumed was a kind of teleportation, but Maria had no way of knowing if DuPris had been referring to the power Max possessed.

Then Maria silenced her chattering thoughts as she felt her body coming apart. Max was doing his thing.

He was *disassembling* them all, molecule by molecule. For a long moment Maria felt like she was expanding, spreading like smoke dissipates in the air.

A disorienting sensation of vertigo overcame her as she realized she could see *through* the bodies of her friends. The feeling of her molecules drifting away was terrifying. Maria focused on Michael—on feeling his aura brushing against her own in the mixture—and felt calm.

A moment later she couldn't think at all.

Isabel heaved a sigh of relief when she'd reformed in front of the chain deep in the caves. Max

140

had pulled it off. Of course, she'd never doubted him for a moment. Still, it felt very good to have her body back in one piece.

"Good work," Michael said. He patted his body like he needed to make sure he was all there.

"Thanks," Max said, sounding tired. Isabel glanced at him, concerned. Max always seemed so in control of himself that it was easy to overlook how much he gave to their efforts. She was about to ask him how he was holding up but didn't. She knew he was sick of being asked.

"C'mon, you guys," Isabel said, rubbing her chilled hands together. "Let's find the maniacal twit and get this over with."

"Isabel, you never disappoint," Max said with a smile. Isabel grinned back, and Max turned to Adam. "You found this tunnel in the first place. Want to do the honors?"

Adam nodded, his eyes wary and alert as he stepped over the chain.

Maria and Liz flicked on their flashlights as soon as they entered the tunnel. Isabel smiled. She, Adam, Michael, and Max could actually see better in the dark, but she knew the trek was probably scary for her friends. She pulled out the flashlight she'd packed as an afterthought and turned it on to give them more light. Michael did the same.

"Does anyone feel anything?" Adam asked from

the head of the group. "I'm not even getting the little twinges of power this time."

"Not a thing," Michael replied with a slight tremor in his voice.

Isabel could relate. She wasn't looking forward to another shock wave.

"The power surge came from this direction . . . generally," Adam said. "I think I'm going the right way, but I just don't know." He sounded frustrated, as if afraid to let the rest of them down.

"Just keep going," Isabel said. "We'll find him."

"Yeah." Max's voice was right behind her. "We have all night."

"Hey, you guys!" Michael called urgently. "Wait up a sec."

"You felt something?" Max asked.

"No, saw something," Michael said. He shined his flashlight on the damp, loamy path. "Look. Someone's been back here."

In the center of the beam of light was a footprint. Isabel's heart jumped to her throat.

"Good work, Sherlock," Maria joked nervously. "Did you join the Boy Scouts while we weren't looking?"

"It could have been there for a while," Isabel said, glancing at Max. "There's no reason to think it's a fresh print. I've got a feeling stuff goes undisturbed back here for decades . . . maybe centuries."

"But maybe it's a good sign," Liz said, pulling her hair back from her shoulders. "Maybe it's DuPris's footprint." She paused and glanced around. "Or would that be a bad sign?"

Adam knelt down beside the shallow, shoe-shaped indentation on the ground. He reached out his finger and lightly touched the center of the footprint.

Isabel felt a tiny surge of energy as the air over the print began to shimmer. She stepped back uncertainly.

In a tiny shimmer of light a holographic image formed, hovering in the tunnel's darkness like a phantom.

"Oh my God," Isabel said with a gasp. "How did you—" But she didn't finish her sentence. A cold finger of fear traced her spine. The hologram was of Mr. Manes. He was walking through the passage where they were standing.

Isabel looked at her brother and saw a grim expression cross his face as the holographic image dissipated.

"That was *not* a good sign," Maria said.

"What was the Major doing back here?" Liz asked. "Do you think he was looking for DuPris, too?"

"Who knows?" Michael said. "But after finding those chemical weapon plans in his files, Manes is definitely not someone I want to be trapped in a cave with."

A long silence hung in the air, suffocating Isabel like a cloud of thick smoke. One enemy had definitely been here. And the other—DuPris—might be very close, too.

"Do we keep going?" Max asked finally.

"We have to," Isabel said, swallowing her fear. The only route toward rescuing Alex was forward, and for him she could face her demons. Even if one of those demons was his own father.

"We might as well follow the footprints," Max said, looking at Isabel. "If the Major *was* looking for DuPris, he may lead us right to him."

"Oh, yay," Maria muttered.

"Let's go," Michael said.

Carefully Adam resumed picking his way through the convoluted passageways, following Mr. Manes's path. The caves felt infinitely more threatening to Isabel now . . . now that she knew a Clean Slate agent was somewhere up ahead.

Adam led them through a series of narrow fissures, and then they emerged into a larger cave. For a moment Isabel was glad for the open space.

But then she gasped as a sharp pain sliced through her heart like a saw. Isabel crumpled to the damp ground as fear clenched her lungs. Her throat burned, and she could barely breathe.

Isabel smelled something acidic. Fumes.

Vaguely, through her disorientation, she heard the painful, horrifying sound of Max choking next to her. She looked around wildly but could focus on nothing.

"It's the chemical weapon!" she heard Liz cry from somewhere far, far above her. Liz's voice sounded like it was spinning away, falling into the distance. "We have to get them out of here!"

And then Isabel heard no more.

TEN

For a split second Liz stood in horrified shock as Adam, Max, Isabel, and Michael crumpled to the ground, one by one. It was like something out of a nightmare, watching their eyes roll back and their bodies go limp as if someone had sucked the life right out of them.

Then Maria screamed, and Liz snapped into crisis control mode. If she and Maria were still standing, the chemical weapon Adam had discovered must be at work. Liz had to help her friends—*now*. She'd always wondered what she would have done if she'd been there when her sister, Rosa, overdosed, and now she knew. There was no way she was going to lose her friends, too, not if she could help it.

"Grab Max's leg," Liz barked at Maria. "We need to drag him to clean air."

Maria was obviously panicked, but she responded to the authority in Liz's voice and did as she was told.

Liz backed up as fast as she could while towing Max. She and Maria back-stepped up the passage they'd come down. Liz hoped that pulling Max to an elevation higher than the ceiling of the poisoned room would keep him safe. She knew most gases were pretty easily trapped at their own level, and she could only pray that the chemical weapon's fumes acted the same way.

For good measure they dragged Max through a few of the fissures in the cave walls that they'd passed on their way in.

Liz had no way of knowing if he would be all right now as she laid him out on the ground. The gas was odorless and colorless, and it didn't affect her at all. Max could be sucking it into his lungs right now.

She stared at Max for a long moment, waiting to see if he'd come to.

"Liz," Maria said, her voice low and urgent.

Liz jerked her head away from Max. She had to leave him. "Let's go," Liz said. She raced back to the others, her flashlight beam bouncing wildly as she ran.

"Isabel next," she called as she scrambled through one of the fissures.

"But Michael might—," Maria began, her voice cracking with emotion.

"No buts," Liz replied sharply without looking back. "We're pulling them out in order of danger, and Max was the weakest. Michael is stronger than Isabel, and Adam is stronger than all of them put together. Case closed." Adam's powers were certainly stronger than the rest of her friends'. She could only hope her assumption about his stamina was right.

When she burst into the room where they'd left the others, Liz ordered herself to focus on Isabel. Only Isabel. The only way to get through this was to decide on an action and not think about anything else. Not Max. Not Adam. Not anything.

She dashed to Isabel's side, crouched down, grabbed her ankles. Maria had Isabel's wrists a second later. And they were moving. Through the passage. Through the cracks in the cave wall. And over to Max.

The second Isabel was on the ground, Liz jerked her focus to Michael, flying back through the fissures, flying back down the passage, flying over to Michael's side. She ignored the burning in her lungs. Ignored the pain in her shoulder where an outcropping of stone had ripped through her shirt and what felt like a couple of layers of skin.

All that mattered now was Michael.

"Hurry, hurry," Maria cried as she grabbed Michael's feet. Liz tried to obey. But Michael was heavy, and it felt like it took years to maneuver him to the spot next to Isabel.

"Only one more to go," Liz called as she started back through the first fissure. Maria gave a grunt in response.

Adam, Liz thought as she ran. Adam, Adam, Adam. His name thudded through her brain with every footfall until she reached him.

Her shoulder screamed in protest as she grabbed Adam under the armpits and hoisted him.

She ignored the pain as she and Maria half carried, half dragged Adam back to the others.

When Adam was in place beside Michael on the cold, dank floor, Liz fell to her knees beside Max. She was gasping for breath as she touched his face.

"Wake up, Max! Please!" she said, taking his hand with both of her own. There was no response, and Max's hand was as cold as ice. Liz's heart slammed to a stop. He couldn't be—

Max gasped for breath, his eyes opening. Liz burst into tears of relief.

Isabel started to sit up, and Michael stirred slowly. Liz quickly kissed Max's forehead and went to check on Adam.

He wasn't breathing.

"Oh my God," Liz choked out. They'd left him down there too long. They hadn't been fast enough. She held her ear to his chest, knowing with an awful certainty that she would hear no heartbeat.

Please, please, prove me wrong, she prayed. For a long moment she heard nothing but silence in his body. Then Liz picked out a faint, irregular thump.

She held her fingers up in front of his mouth and nose. He still wasn't breathing. He needed mouth-to-mouth resuscitation or he would die.

Without a moment of hesitation Liz pressed Adam's nostrils closed with two fingers and covered his soft mouth with her own.

* * *

Adam woke to the bizarre feeling of his lungs being inflated by three short puffs of breath.

Then he realized that Liz's lips were pressed against his own. He didn't know why. He didn't know how it happened. All he knew was . . . soft. Liz's lips were so soft. He'd thought about Liz's lips a lot, but he'd never realized how soft they would feel.

How would they taste? Would they taste the way he'd imagined? He flicked his tongue across her bottom lip, and Liz pulled away, startled.

Adam sat up dizzily, not ready to give up the contact with Liz. She leaned forward, hugging him tightly. "I thought you were dead," she said softly.

Adam buried his face in her hair and hugged her back. "Are you okay?" Liz asked, pulling back to look into his eyes.

Adam tried to nod, which wasn't a great idea. His head was flooded with darkness the moment he moved, but it faded. Through his shaky vision he could see Max, Isabel, and Michael struggling to their feet behind Liz. "What . . . what happened?" Adam asked.

Liz smiled and rubbed his arm gently, which made Adam feel like curling up against her warm body and going to sleep.

"My guess is that you guys got a good dose of that chemical weapon you read about in the Major's files," she answered.

"That's a good guess," Max added softly.

Michael stood up, rubbing his temples. "Well, we've found out that the weapon works," he said ruefully. "I was out before I even knew what hit me."

Isabel coughed harshly. "Ugh!" she cried. "That's a taste I could do without."

Adam still felt pretty ill himself, but his head was starting to clear. "You saved us?" he asked Liz. His heart lurched. "You pulled us away from the gas?"

"Well, Maria and I did," she said, her eyes meeting his quickly, then flicking away.

Max shuffled over to Liz and wrapped his arms around her. She clung to him, closing her eyes tightly. Adam forced himself to look away. He didn't need to torture himself.

"What now?" Max asked the group.

"We go home, right?" Maria said. "You beam us out of here, and we all go home until you've recovered enough to try again."

"I say we keep going," Isabel countered. "This might be our only chance to get to DuPris. We have to do this for Alex."

"You almost *died*," Maria reminded her.

"Not for the first time," Isabel shot back. Her words sounded tough, but Adam could see from the bleached white squiggles in her purple aura that she was terrified of what lay ahead.

"And probably not for the last time, either," Michael added. "I, for one, want Alex back here as soon as possible. I say we go ahead."

"I'm with you guys," Max said. "That gas is quick, but its effects don't seem to linger very long. I say we go for it."

"Yeah," Liz said. "Let's get this over with."

"Adam?" Max asked. "What do you want to do?"

A shot of guilt struck Adam like a shovel. Max was treating him like an equal, and all Adam could think about was getting him out of the way. At least far enough out of the way that Adam could taste Liz's lips again.

"Let's go get DuPris," Adam said, looking Max in the eye. "And the Major. They've gotten away with enough."

"Fine," Maria piped up. "I'm not going to be the only holdout here. Let's go get Alex back."

Adam led again as they searched for another, untainted passage through the jagged maze of hollowed-out, intertwined tunnels. Maybe it was because he'd spent his life wandering down the labyrinthine corridors of the Clean Slate compound, but Adam didn't hesitate as he forged ahead.

As Adam scrambled over a wide, convoluted mass of hardened limestone deposits, he felt it again—the violent surge of power that had knocked him senseless back in the Painted Grotto. But this time he was prepared for the torrent of energy and closed his mind to it before it could hurt him again.

He glanced back to see how the others had fared. Isabel, Max, and Michael looked pained and weakened, but they had weathered the intense flood.

"It's close," Adam said.

"Very close," Max agreed.

Once he had cleared the deposit of limestone, Adam ran toward the source of the surge, the others keeping close behind.

Then he stopped in his tracks. He'd hit a dead end.

"It's this way," Adam said. "I know it is."

"We need to go through the wall," Michael said. "You guys feel strong enough?"

"Let's connect," Isabel suggested.

Adam held out his hands to Max and Isabel, and Michael took Isabel's other hand. Their connection was forged as easily as if they'd been doing it their whole lives.

Ready? Adam asked.

Ready, came the reply.

They had to be careful not to blast away too much, or the cave ceiling would come tumbling down and bury them all. Adam used his trained skills to focus their energy down to a single beam of pure force. They collected their power for a moment, building up a reservoir.

Now! Adam ordered. They released the built-up beam at the center of the cave wall.

The explosion was deafening. Clouds of dust and debris billowed around them, and for a second the only sense of his surroundings Adam had was the pressure on his hands from Max and Isabel.

Finally Adam's ears stopped ringing and the dust settled.

"The ship," Isabel exclaimed.

And there it was. The ship was docked directly in front of them, its otherworldly metal hull shimmering and rippling. It looked as unreal and out of place as an animated cartoon character walking down the main strip of Roswell.

Adam dropped Isabel's and Max's hands and started toward it. But then he saw something that made his heart freeze in fury and fear.

Elsevan DuPris was standing across the room, glaring at them. The Stone of Midnight was glowing in his hand.

"Mr. Manes!" Liz shouted.

"What?" Adam asked. He turned around to see what Liz was talking about.

It was the man from the hologram—the Major. Adam watched in horror as Liz hurled herself at him and grabbed the Major's arm, struggling with the man, who was twice her size.

Adam didn't hesitate. He ran straight toward Liz.

"Adam, no!" Liz screamed as the Major pushed her out of the way.

It was only then that Adam noticed that the Major was pointing a taser at Adam's chest.

A bright flash of white light blinded Adam just as he realized that Liz had been trying to save his life—again.

And then everything went black.

ELEVEN

Michael watched in shock as Adam crumpled to the ground, smoke rising from his chest. Slowly he raised his chin to glare at his two greatest enemies, wondering which to go after first.

DuPris, an alien like himself, with no sense of decency or honor, or even right or wrong.

Or the Major. An agent of Project Clean Slate, dedicated to eradicating alien life on earth.

He wanted them both. But Adam was down. For now that was all that mattered. Michael rushed over to Adam and knelt beside him. He had to connect now.

Confused shouting filled the large cave, but Michael blocked it all out and concentrated on joining himself with Adam. He felt the pulse of Adam's blood, and he shifted his energy to match Adam's aura.

He was in; he and Adam were one. Now all Michael had to do was repair the damage the Major's taser had done to Adam's body. *Their* body.

And hope Mr. Manes didn't decide to fire that taser at him.

* * *

The collective consciousness roiled with venomous rage at the sight of DuPris. For a moment Max was scared that the consciousness would surge forward in his mind and take control of him once again . . . like the time he'd encountered DuPris in their cave.

Max waited for the overwhelming rush of force of the consciousness taking him over, but it didn't come. For whatever reason, they remained separate. Although they still filled Max's mind with furious, violent images that he was afraid to inspect too closely.

Isabel stepped up behind him. Max knew she was ready to join powers with him. But it wouldn't be enough. With Michael, Adam, Liz, and Maria it might be enough. But just him and Isabel. Forget about it.

DuPris raised one eyebrow, as if he knew exactly what Max was thinking. Then he casually glanced to his left, toward the sound of footsteps pounding across the cave floor.

Max followed DuPris's gaze and saw Mr. Manes running toward DuPris.

"I wish I could take the time to play with all of you," DuPris said, "but I just have too much to do today." He raised his hand, the Stone glowing purplegreen in his fingers.

"No!" Mr. Manes yelled, lurching forward in an obvious attempt to grab the Stone. But he was too late.

The Stone of Midnight flashed, and Max found himself flying through the air. Literally flying. He sailed across the long cave toward the ship, too startled to even scream.

Out of the corner of his eye Max saw Liz tumbling through the air, too. Her hair covered her face like a flapping veil.

In front of him a portal gaped open in the side of the ship, just in time for him to fly through it. Max somersaulted once and landed hard on the seamless metal floor of the ship's interior.

A split second later Liz rocketed through the door and crashed into Max, knocking the wind out of him.

"Are you hurt?" Max asked breathlessly. Liz shook her head, and Max struggled to get out from under her, but before he could extricate himself, Isabel came flying through the door, too, followed by Adam, Michael, and Maria. They landed in a tangled heap atop Max and Liz as the portal swirled shut—without leaving so much as a seam.

In the moment of calm that followed, Max managed to pull himself to a sitting position. Isabel shifted, and suddenly Max's heart gave a painful kick. Mr. Manes was sitting right behind Isabel. DuPris had thrown him in with the rest of them.

"You're dead!" Michael shouted, scrambling across the ship and hurling himself onto the Major. "You tried to kill Adam—you die!"

"I didn't mean to—"

"Shut up!" Michael shouted.

He frisked the guy, Mr. Manes not making any

attempt to stop him, and came up with a small metal canister. Michael tossed it to Max.

Max caught the canister as Michael pulled back his fist, aiming for the Major's face.

"Stop!" Max shouted.

Michael froze.

Max scrambled to his feet. "That's Alex's dad you're about to pound on," he told Michael, his voice sounding unnaturally calm to his ears. "You might want to reconsider."

"Why?" Michael shot back. "He's a Clean Slate agent . . . and he just tried to kill Adam!"

The Major cleared his throat. "Can I say something here—"

"No!" Max and Michael both shouted at the same time.

"You should probably just shut up," Isabel added.

At that moment Max's ears rang with a huge metallic crunching sound and the floor convulsed. He had to sidestep to stay on his feet. His eyes widened as he realized that the *walls* had just shifted closer, making the space in the ship significantly smaller.

Almost immediately another resounding crunch shook the ship. And again the walls closed in. The floor buckled under Max, and this time he was thrown to the ground.

"DuPris is crushing the ship," Adam said in a tired voice. "He's compressing it with his mind."

Michael released the Major and scrambled to the center of the room, turning from side to side to study the walls. "It's okay," he said. "Nothing can hurt this material."

"Yeah. The ship always returns to its original shape," Adam added.

Isabel laughed frantically. "Oh, goody," she said. "That's nice for the ship. But if you think for a *second*, you might notice that by the time it does, we're going to be nothing but ugly splats on the floor! Or the ceiling!"

Everyone in the ship was struck silent for a moment, realizing the horrible truth of Isabel's words.

"Or both," Maria said.

"So what do you propose we do?" Michael asked Isabel.

"We bust out of here," she answered instantly. "We blast a big hole in the wall and get the hell out!"

"We can't hurt this metal," Michael told her. "It's made for intergalactic travel. I don't think we can compete with that."

"DuPris opened the wall," Liz said. "So it's possible."

"Yeah," Michael said. "Possible if you have the Stone of Midnight."

"Well, we have to do *something*," Isabel shot back as the walls crunched ever closer. "I'm not going to just sit here until DuPris squishes us like snails. We can at least *try*. Let's link up."

Adam hurried over, and Isabel grabbed his hand and Michael's. Max hooked up with Adam, and then they were one unit again, a single force with the power of all four of them combined.

Isabel concentrated. She imagined the side of the ship, pictured its shiny, shimmering wall, and then she pictured that same wall with a big hole in it. They *urged* the molecules of the wall to separate, to stretch, to stand aside. It was exhausting. The alien metal was stronger than anything Isabel had dealt with before.

Then she felt a slight give in the wall's integrity. A space opened, about as big as a pea.

Wider, Isabel screamed. Wider!

But the hole slid closed without leaving a mark.

Isabel groaned in frustration.

"We need more power," Adam said.

"Maria?" Max asked. "Liz?"

Without any hesitation they rushed over and joined the circle.

This time the six of them managed to open a hole the size of a quarter.

Which closed again almost immediately.

The ship crunched again. Isabel could now touch both walls at once with her outstretched hands. "What are we going to do?" she cried.

"If you can open that hole again," Mr. Manes said, "I might have a solution."

Isabel turned to glare at the Major. As if he even had a right to speak! "We don't need help from you!"

"C'mon, Isabel," Maria shouted. "He doesn't want to be smushed, either!"

"What is it?" Max asked.

"If you can open that hole again, I could activate a chemical weapon and aim it out the hole into the cavern," Mr. Manes said. "That should take care of DuPris."

"Not a bad plan," Michael said. "Maybe even a decent plan. But I'll be the one to activate that canister, not you. I'm not going to risk you killing us all."

The Major swallowed hard. "The weapon is keyed to my DNA," he told Michael. "It won't function for anyone but me."

Another forceful crunch rocked the ship as DuPris squeezed it like a lemon from the outside. Isabel noticed with alarm that the ceiling was now pressing down against Max's head.

"He's already tried to kill us once with the gas that comes out of that thing," Isabel yelled.

"I didn't know you were in the caverns," Mr. Manes protested. "Those weren't set for you—I placed them around DuPris's cave so that he couldn't escape. . . ."

The Major's voice trailed off, and he paused a moment before speaking again. "Wait a minute," he said. "If those weapons worked on you . . . and all this talk about 'linking up'. . ."

"So you've figured us out," Isabel said. "Good for you. But I know the truth about you, too, Mr. Clean Slate. At least we don't go rounding people up in order to lock them away . . . or kill them!"

The Major blinked at Isabel, looking confused. "What do you mean?" he asked. "It has never been Clean Slate's agenda to—"

The ship quaked again, knocking them all to the floor. Isabel gasped as Max got back on his feet. He could no longer stand upright. There were now less than five feet between the floor and the ceiling.

At that moment panic overtook Isabel's indignation. If they trusted the Major, they could die. But if they didn't trust him, they'd definitely die.

Once again the ship let out a metallic squeal as DuPris compressed it further. Isabel was thrown onto Adam, and she didn't bother getting up again. There was no place for her to go. The walls around them were so close now, it was painful just to be in the ship. There was no time left.

"Let's just do it!" Isabel shouted.

Max handed the canister to Major Manes, and all Isabel could do now was hope that they'd made the right decision.

Quickly Isabel grabbed Michael's leg, and Adam grabbed Max's arm. Maria and Liz were already connected through Max. Together they opened a hole large enough for the end of the canister.

Mr. Manes thrust the tip of the weapon through

the hole and squirted a long stream of chemicals into the cavern outside.

He pulled the spent canister back in just as the group could hold the hole open no longer.

Isabel slumped against Adam, feeling more drained than she'd ever felt before. They were in here. The chemicals and DuPris were out there.

Now all they could do was wait.

And hope.

Max waited. He waited for the crunch of the ship that would let them know they hadn't been successful in neutralizing DuPris. The final crunch that would end their lives.

Then a thought struck him—a disturbing thought. Something none of them had even considered.

DuPris had opened the wall of the ship and jammed them inside. If the chemical killed DuPris and the walls stopped closing in, who would let them out?

Panic started to squeeze Max's heart the same way DuPris had crushed the ship—in sudden, painful jolts.

But then, miraculously, the walls of the ship began to fade.

Max climbed onto his knees, peering at the wall closest to him. It definitely seemed less substantial than it had a moment before. It was becoming transparent!

It was dissolving.

In less than a minute the ship had melted away, leaving Max, Liz, Isabel, Michael, Maria, Adam, and the Major lying on the slick floor of the cavern.

"The gas!" Isabel cried, sitting up. "Is it still in the air?"

"Don't worry," Mr. Manes said. "I only used a minuscule amount. It should have dissipated by now."

Max took a deep breath and glanced quickly around the cave.

DuPris was nowhere to be seen. He had vanished.

Taking the ship with him.

Max's first reaction was disbelief. DuPris was unbelievably strong. He had survived the chemicals and managed to transport himself away with the ship. How were they ever supposed to fight someone that powerful?

A cold wash of disappointment flooded Max. Without the ship, their chance at saving Alex had vanished, too.

DuPris could have transported himself—and the ship—to anywhere on earth. Maybe DuPris was even strong enough to teleport someplace off the planet . . . like the moon.

Alex was trapped until they found DuPris again or until the collective consciousness recovered their strength enough to open another wormhole. But by that time Alex could already be dead.

"What do we do now?" Maria asked Max.

He was the one who always got asked questions like that. He was the one his friends turned to. "I have no idea," he admitted, forcing himself to look at her as he answered.

"What does that do?" Adam asked.

At first Max thought Adam was talking to him. Then he realized Adam's question was for Mr. Manes.

Max turned toward the Major. He had a shiny, copper-colored ball in his hand. As Max watched, he gently placed it on the floor of the cave.

"The orb, that is, this little ball here, has the ability to store and magnify power used in its presence," Mr. Manes explained. "More specifically, power thrown off by that stone DuPris had in his possession."

Mr. Manes swallowed. He now had Max's full attention, and Max was sure that all his friends were listening as intently as he was.

"It might have stored up enough power now to bring Alex home," the Major said.

Max blinked at Alex's father. The Major knew where Alex was. That surprised Max so much, he was left speechless.

"How do you turn it on?" Liz asked, pointing at the ball. "Or use it. Whatever."

"Like this," Mr. Manes replied. With a flick of his wrist he set the ball spinning on the cavern floor. And then he scuttled back out of the way.

After the initial force to get it started, Max noticed that the ball spun faster and faster under its own power, seemingly in defiance of several basic laws of physics.

Max couldn't take his eyes off the spinning orb as it began to whirl so rapidly, it was nothing but a coppery blur.

Then it began to throw off sparks.

Dazzling lights surrounded the ball, also whirling in some intricate dance of their own. With the brilliant satellites swirling around it, the ball reminded Max of an atom and its electrons. Or the planets revolving around a star.

Something began to form in the air over the gyrating orb. A whirling haze of molecules.

Max squinted, trying to bring the fuzzy shape into focus.

It was an image.

An image of Alex.

Max felt Liz take his hand, and he gave her hand a soft squeeze in response. He couldn't stop staring at the image sharpening over the spinning, sparkling, luminous ball.

The image was growing stronger—clearer—with every passing second. And it wasn't just a hologram. Those were physical, solid molecules gathering above the ball. It wasn't merely made of light.

The ball—whatever it was—was bringing Alex back.

Excitement rose in Max's throat like a bird trapped in a chimney. It was going to work! Alex was coming home!

But then the ball began to slow down.

Mr. Manes let out a pained growl from deep in his chest as the ball developed a wobble. The image of Alex began to fade.

"No!" Max shouted. "Don't let it stop. Connect, everybody connect now!"

Max was already holding hands with Liz, so he reached out with his free hand and clamped onto Isabel's arm. In less than a second all six of them had once again formed their thrilling, essential union.

They were one.

Send everything we've got at the ball, Max instructed the group. Send it all! Keep it spinning! Keep it spinning!

For a moment Alex's image became clear and crisp. His eyes moved from Isabel to Max to Liz, and Max was sure that Alex saw them. Saw them!

But then the image flickered.

And winked out.

ROSWELL HIGH

SIX TEENS,
ONE SECRET . . .

Max loves **Liz**, but he can't let her get too close . . .

Alex wants **Isabel**—but is she just using him?

Maria always daydreams about **Michael**. But will he ever stop thinking of her as a little sister?

Don't miss the next Roswell High:

THE REBEL

Michael has finally found the one thing he always yearned for—family. When his brother, Trevor, arrives in Roswell, Michael will do anything to please him. But soon, Trevor's loyalties come into question—and Michael is caught in the cross fire.

Maria's little brother has disappeared and she knows the kidnappers are trying to get to her and her friends. Devastated and guilt-ridden, Maria turns to Michael for help. But will he be there for her, or has Michael himself become the enemy?

Look for Roswell High #9,
THE DARK ONE
Coming soon!

. . . A GIRL BORN
WITHOUT THE FEAR GENE

FEARLESS™

A NEW SERIES BY
FRANCINE PASCAL

A TITLE AVAILABLE EVERY MONTH

From Pocket Pulse
Published by Pocket Books

Dawson's Creek ™

**Look for more new,
original Dawson's Creek™ stroies
wherever books are sold.**

And don't miss:

Dawson's Creek™
The Official Postcard Book

Dawson's Creek™
The Official Scrapbook

Available now from Pocket Pulse
Published by Pocket Books

**Visit Pocket Books on the World Wide Web
http://www.SimonSays.com**

**Visit the Sony website at
*http://www.dawsonscreeek.com***

Bullying.
Threats.
Bullets.

Locker
searches?
Metal
detectors?

Fight back without fists.

fight for your rights:
take a stand against violence